SMALL SPACE LIVING

XPERT TIPS AND TECHNIQUES ON USING CLOSETS, CORNERS, AND EVERY OTHER SPACE IN YOUR HOME

ROBERTA SANDENBERGH

ARCHITECT AIA

Skyhorse Publishing

Skyhorse Publishing books may be purchased in bulk at special discounts for sales promotion, corporate gifts, fund-raising, or educational purposes. Special editions can also be created to specifications. For details, contact the Special Sales Department, Skyhorse Publishing, 307 West 36th Street, 11th Floor, New York, NY 10018 or info@skyhorsepublishing.com.

Skyhorse® and Skyhorse Publishing® are registered trademarks of Skyhorse Publishing, Inc.®, a Delaware corporation.

Visit our website at www.skyhorsepublishing.com.

10 9 8 7 6 5 4 3 2 1

Library of Congress Cataloging-in-Publication Data is available on file.

Cover design by Mona Lin
Cover photos: top—courtesy of MAFF Apartments The Hague. Design: Queeste Architects; bottom left—courtesy of Hamish Niven, photographer. Design by Roberta Sandenbergh, Interior by Sager & Associates; bottom center—illustration by hafiz Omer Shafiq; and bottom right—Design by Kathleen Kelly for Parador.

Book design by Alun Davies
Small Space Architect logo design credit: Johan Dreyer

Print ISBN: 978-1-5107-3631-3
Ebook ISBN: 978-1-5107-3632-0

Printed in China

CHAPTER 5

STACKED SPACES: "DON'T FORGET THE VERTICAL DIMENSION."

IDEA#

CHAPTER 6

WALL SPACES: "A WALL IS MORE THAN A SPACE DIVIDER." — 125

IDEA#

CHAPTER 9

CHAPTER 10

INTRODUCTION

When I was eleven, I had the chance to design my own bedroom when we were about to move into a new house. I measured all my books, all my toys, and all my clothes. Everything had to fit exactly into the new bedroom. It was the start of my career in small-space living. From my childhood bedroom to my tiny dorm room in college, to the studio apartment where I live today, I have always loved carving out small cozy "nests" to live in.

Travel in a Camper Van

In my twenties, I lived with my architect husband in a small one-bedroom apartment in Greenwich Village where we used every last inch of the 800-square-foot space. We built shallow cabinets and closets to hang on the walls and even fit our new baby into a closet and our drawing boards into the kitchen.

When we decided to travel around Europe in a camper, we renovated a VW van so that a kitchen folded down in the back, a seat slid out to become a double bed, and a box under the front seat became a place for our four-year-old daughter's sleeping bag. For almost two years, the three of us lived very happily in this tiny, 80-square-foot van, which we named Daisy Belle.

In my thirties, when I found myself a widow living in South Africa, I divided a thatch-roof house into two small cottages, one to live in and one to rent out for extra income. Later on, I converted the garage into another small cottage. I chose to live in these small spaces even though it wasn't absolutely necessary. My daughter and I lived in a small 700-square-foot cottage on an enormous 11-acre property!

In my fifties, I renovated a small beach apartment in Cape Town, South Africa, at first adding a curtain to create a second bedroom and then extending it to create a third bedroom and a second bathroom—all in 1,050 square feet (98 m²).

I eventually moved back to New York and was lucky enough to find an apartment I could divide in two, so I could afford to live there again. I now live in a studio apartment in the heart of Manhattan where small-space living is a necessity because every square inch of space costs a small fortune. But, even if that were not the case, I would still treasure every last inch of my little apartment and not want it to be any bigger.

Throughout the book, I tell the stories of all the places I have designed and lived in—and, along the way, offer ideas for you, my readers, to adapt for your own homes.

MY DESIGN METHOD

Over the years—for myself and for my clients—I have developed a "nose" for space. I can almost smell a hidden space. So you might call my design method a form of detective work. I examine a house or apartment to see if there are any untapped places where I could possibly gain even the smallest amount of extra space. I look at the closets, the walls and windows, even the floor and ceiling in the hope of finding underused, poorly used, or even empty spaces. Then I look for ways to maximize these spaces and use them more efficiently. And that's where the fun comes in. When I am able to find more usable living space in a home, I can assure you it is a very joyful experience!

SPACE OPPORTUNITIES

I have deliberately avoided organizing this book according to types of rooms. You will not find here "Small-Space Bedroom Ideas" or "Small-Space Kitchen Ideas." Rather, I have divided the book into chapters by what I call "Space Opportunities." These opportunities exist in every room of your home. You just have to look for them.

TAKE A TOUR OF YOUR HOME

Here you are—moving into a new house or apartment or looking to expand your existing home. Maybe you have a new baby. Maybe you want to start working from home. You need more space, and you don't know where to start. What I advise you to do is take a tour of your home and look at it with new eyes as if you have never seen it before.

If you have a high ceiling, that's a no-brainer. You can easily create an extra bedroom, an art studio, or a home office in a loft. But even spaces with low ceiling heights can be doubled up—especially over closets, entry areas, kitchens, and bathrooms.

Then look at your closets. Do you really need all the stuff in them? Maybe you could get rid of some of it. Or put it somewhere else. As you will see in this book, I'm a big fan of drawers under beds, shelves above doors, and shallow cabinet/closets on walls. In these days of tiny gadgets, an empty closet can become your home office. In our brave new world of online meal deliveries, it could easily become a kitchen. Or even a baby's room. Start thinking small.

The same goes for window recesses. I have used them for a dressing table, a Murphy bed, a desk, and even a bathtub. Walls, floors, and ceilings can also be put to good use. You get the picture.

Photo by John Sandenbergh.

Baby in a Closet

You just have to look around for "space opportunities," such as:

- High ceilings
- Excess closets
- Window recesses
- Wall recesses
- Corners
- Empty walls

- Empty spaces
- Unused spaces
- Rarely used spaces
- Duplicate spaces
- Staircases

After taking the tour, ask yourself what you really need and want in your home:

- Which spaces do you enjoy most?
- Where do you spend the most amount of time?
- Where do you spend the least amount of time?
- What do you think you need less of?
- What do you think you need more of?
- What would you like to change?
- How would you like to live?
- Where and how do you think you can expand your space?

And answer some specific questions:

- Where do you work on your computer?
- Could you sleep on a smaller bed?
- Could you use a Murphy bed?
- How often do you eat in your dining room?
- How much do you cook?
- Could you use a smaller kitchen?
- How often do you entertain?

Using a High Ceiling

Photo by Roberta Sandenbergh.

MY SMALL-SPACE RULES

1. If you don't need something or love it, get rid of it.
2. Find a dedicated place for everything you own so it belongs somewhere and you don't waste time looking for it.
3. Make every activity like dining or working feel separate, even within a larger space.
4. Always shop with a tape measure and measure carefully before you buy.
5. Make everything fit exactly.
6. Don't be afraid of the word *custom-made* if you can't find something "ready-made" that fits your space. Sites like homeadvisor.com and angieslist.com steer you to recommended carpenters and handymen. Or you may be able to do it yourself. (Some stores like Home Depot cut shelves and boards to size.)
7. Remember that the gain is worth the pain and that (after a while) you won't miss your old spread-out lifestyle.
8. And always remember that space is money!

CLOSET SPACES

If you have a closet, you have an extra room.

Real Estate Investment

Closets are rooms. Valuable real estate! A typical 42"x 24" (1067mm x 610mm) closet in a Manhattan apartment that might sell for $1,800 a square foot is worth $12,600!

That's just one closet. Multiply it by all the others in your house or apartment, and you will be horrified at how much you are paying for a bunch of stuff you hardly ever—or worse, NEVER—use.

Build a Fantasy

I think people like me who live in small apartments have a common fantasy. We wake up one morning, open a door, and lo and behold: there's an extra room! Suddenly, we have a study or even a guest room. It's an urban dream.

You can stop dreaming. That room already exists. The trouble is it's full of old bridesmaid dresses, ski outfits from a trip you took five years ago, and a whole bunch of clothes that don't fit you anymore.

Step One

The message is: lose the junk and expand your life. Get rid of, or at the very least pack away, the stuff you don't need or love.

After the Salvation Army makes its pickup and your bridesmaid dresses are in boxes under your bed, you will have an EMPTY closet. Then, instead of going out and buying more stuff to fill it up again, make it into an extra room. How about a home office, a kitchen, or even a room for a baby?

Step Two

Hire a handyman. You don't need a fancy carpenter to convert a closet. A handy husband, the handyman in your building, or someone you find at angieslist.com or homeadvisor.com will all do fine.

BABY IN A CLOSET

Don't be in a hurry to move.

A baby is very small and certainly doesn't need a whole room. My advice is to make do with whatever space you have. You have enough to worry about with a new baby; you don't need the extra stress of moving. Consider using a closet. Just take off the doors.

Don't Mind What People Say

People may think it strange to put a baby in a closet. Some will be horrified. They will make jokes. Explain that you've taken off the doors and stand your ground.

How-To Tips:

It is a lot of work organizing a baby closet—and even more keeping it tidy. But don't give up. It can be the perfect little home for your little baby. And you can put off moving for quite a while.

(a) First Measure the Door Opening

A closet with a 36" (914mm) door is ideal because it is the same length as a normal crib. If your closet door is only 24" (610mm), it will be challenging but still doable, so long as the inside of the closet is at least 36" (914mm). A closet with double doors is best because the extra room gives you a diaper-changing space next to the crib (b).

Courtesy of Skip Hop

(b) Add a Diaper-Changing Area

If you have the room, put this next to the crib. It should be a little higher than the crib. Buy a ready-made plastic changing pad with a strap. Then hang up a shoe bag on the wall for all the stuff like baby wipes, baby oil, and talcum powder—plus a trash bag to hold the diapers as they come off. A waste bin takes up too much space, and you could trip over it.

(c) Make It Look like A Baby Room

Hang a valance from the doorframe. Hang a mobile from the ceiling. Make a colorful design on the wall with cutouts. All these add-ons tell the world: "This is not a closet. It's a baby room."

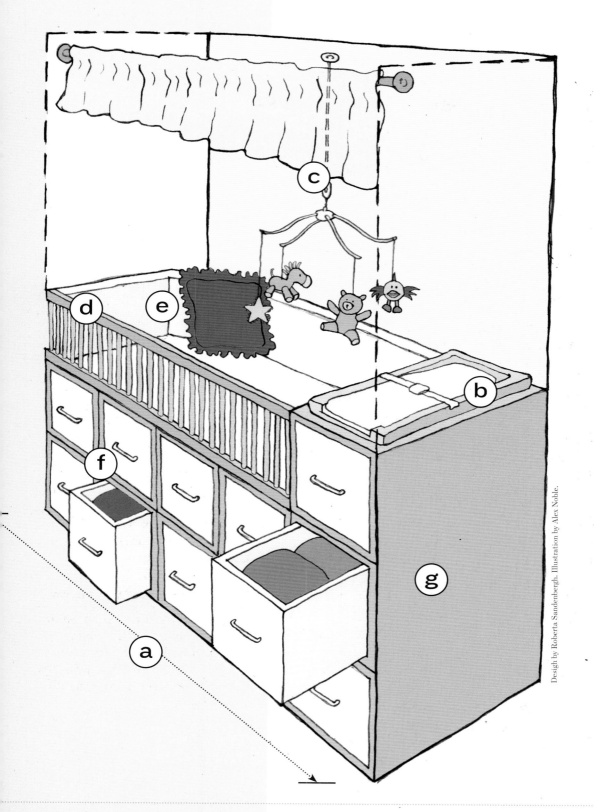

(d) Install a Crib Rail

You don't have to build in a wood crib rail that attaches to the wall. I recommend using a metal rail that is usually meant for toddler beds, like the one shown here from *Dream On Me*. Just attach it very securely to the base underneath the mattress and buy a rail cover so the baby doesn't hurt its head.

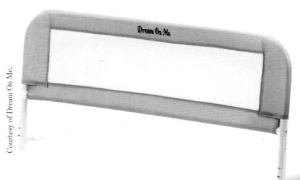

Courtesy of Dream On Me.

(e) Add a Mattress and a Bumper

Buy a standard portable crib-size mattress and a three-sided crib bumper.

(f) Lots of Drawers Underneath

Your baby may be small, but it comes with an enormous amount of baggage. The disposable diapers alone can overwhelm an apartment. Then come the baby clothes and towels and blankets—not to mention toys. I found that double-stacked letter-size file drawers (24" x 12" x 10"; 610mm x 305mm x 254mm) are ideal. I recommend the heavy-duty cardboard file drawers that are meant for archives. They come folded, usually six to a pack. Decorate the fronts with bright colors. And after your baby outgrows the closet, you can use them for your own file storage.

(g) Build a Crib Base

Order a 3/4" (19mm)-thick piece of plywood the exact dimensions of the inside of the closet. Use an edging strip in front. The closet walls may be a bit skew, so you might need a side molding to cover a gap. Install the board at a convenient height—convenient for you, not the baby. The baby won't care if its bed is higher or lower than a normal crib. The higher it is, the less you have to bend and the more drawers you can fit underneath.

MY STORY

My architect husband, John, and I, newly married and very ambitious, renovated a one-bedroom apartment on lower Fifth Avenue in Greenwich Village in New York City. We did the work ourselves and were just about finished when we found out I was pregnant. We were so in love with our magnificent apartment with its high ceilings and arched windows that we didn't even consider moving. We just had to figure out where to put the baby. We had only one bedroom, but it had a very big closet, at least by New York standards: 60" (1524mm) long and 30" (762mm) deep—ideal for a baby room! We designed a built-in crib bed with a guardrail and room for storage underneath. For storage, we used sturdy cardboard file drawers with colored fronts. We stacked them five in a row, two-high, with an extra stack on the side for a changing area. With a valance and a mobile, this became our daughter's home for the first three-and-a-half years of her life, and it was terrific. Even today, when I show her a picture of the little closet, she gets a dreamy smile on her face. But maybe it's because I have told her about it so many times.

....

P.S. I was one of the first mothers in the 1960s to use disposable diapers, which were very expensive at that time. My mother was horrified. "You're using paper diapers on my grandchild?" she cried. "Yes, mother. I am using paper diapers—and cardboard drawers!"

....

P.P.S. We had to find places to put our own belongings after we lost our one and only closet. So we used the walls. Every inch of wall space in that apartment became a candidate for storage. But that's another story and another chapter. (See Chapter 6, Wall Spaces.)

IDEA 2.

BATHROOM IN A CLOSET
It could save your marriage.

Sharing Can be Stressful
Sharing a bathroom can be stressful, even with your nearest and dearest. A separate bathroom, no matter how small, could be the deciding factor between having and not having a live-in partner.

Note: Not for Large People
A bathroom in a closet will be a small bathroom, a very small bathroom. You may not have to hold your breath and slide in sideways, but you will definitely have to move with care.

Sliding Door
There probably won't be room for a regular swing door. A sliding door is the best option, with or without a wall pocket. A folding door is second best, but only if it has a secure lock.

(a) Step Up
You may have to raise the floor with a step at the door, so the toilet has the necessary slope to drain properly.

(b) Floor Finish
I suggest a nonslip floor like the rubberized matting at swimming pools. No ceramic tiles. You cannot afford to slip and fall in such a small room.

(c) Toilet
A toilet is 19" (483mm) wide and an average person only slightly less. You and the toilet will fit just fine into a 24" (610mm)-wide space, even if there isn't room for a toilet paper holder.

(d) Tank Toilet Paper Holder
You can buy a gizmo to hold toilet paper at the side of the cistern, for multiple or single rolls. It may take a bit of getting used to, but it beats keeping the paper on the floor. This product is a great solution from BHG (Better Homes & Garden), a product sold as a *medium caddy*. Attach it to the side of your toilet cistern and—with no extra wall or floor space required—you now have room for four rolls of toilet paper!

Courtesy of Walmart.

(e) Space above the Toilet
I suggest putting a tissue box right on top of the toilet, a shelf above that for towels, and a cabinet for medical supplies on top.

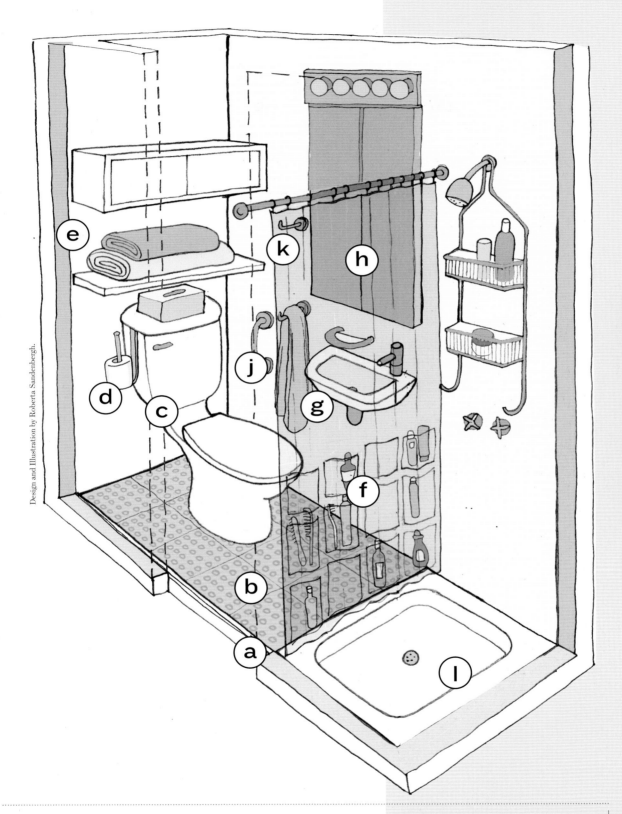

Design and Illustration by Roberta Sandenbergh.

Shower Curtain with Pockets

(f) You can buy shower curtains with pockets to hold stuff. They also offer a little bit of privacy if two (extremely skinny) people should ever use the bathroom at the same time.

Sink Basin

(g) Get the smallest wall-hung wash hand basin you can find. It should protrude no more than 9" (229mm) from the wall. In a 24" (610mm)-deep closet, there will be only 15" (381mm) left over. Holding your breath, you will just about fit.

Space above the Sink

(h) I suggest a medicine cabinet all the way up to the ceiling with mirrored doors and a built-in light. You can't have too much room for toiletries.

Grab Bars

(j) Install a grab bar on the wall near the toilet and another in the shower. Be safe.

Towel Hooks

(k) There probably won't be room for a towel rail, so put up towel hooks next to the sink and at the door. If you have a swing door, you can use a towel hook that replaces the door hinge. There's even one on Amazon that holds multiple towels. A benefit of a towel hook over a towel rail is that you don't have to fold the towels.

Shower curtain photo courtesy of Maytex.

Sink basin photo courtesy of Vilas

Towel hook photo courtesy of OrganizeIt

You can save space and water by using a combination fixture that recycles water from the basin to flush the toilet, thereby saving thousands of liters of water.

There are now several of these on the market. The one shown here is by Alvaro Ares of Spain.

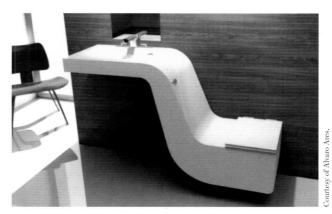

Courtesy of Alvaro Ares.

Toilet-Sink Combo

Shower Pan

The floor part of a shower is called a shower pan. You can order this online. If the standard sizes are too big for your closet, you may have to order a custom size.

Disappearing Shower Door

An ingenious design called OpenSpace from Duravit has a shower door that folds flat against the wall. You can also order it as a mirrored door and make the shower into a dressing room.

Courtesy of Duravit AG.

Ventilation

You will definitely have to install an exhaust fan.

MY STORY

I once renovated a house in Cape Town, South Africa, for a young couple with a new baby. Like many old houses, there was only one bathroom, even with three bedrooms. When the couple hired a nursemaid, it became chaos. Everyone was bumping into one another, and it was clear that they desperately needed a second bathroom, but there was no room to put it. The only "opportunity" space I could find was the one and only closet in the master bedroom, a very long space that ran the full width of the room. The couple finally agreed to sacrifice this wonderful closet in order to turn it into an en-suite bathroom. I designed it with a toilet at one end, a shower at the other, and a narrow sink in the middle, just opposite the doorway. Luckily, the couple was able to find two beautiful antique armoires for their clothes and it was a happy ending all around.

SHOWER IN A CLOSET

Add a shower to a powder room.

Add Value to Your Home

If you own a "1½-bath" apartment and want to upgrade it to "2-bath" status, you may be able to borrow space from an adjoining closet or empty corridor space. The plumbing is already there. The ventilation is there. Besides improving your lifestyle, this renovation is the single best thing you can do to increase the value of your home.

MY STORY

In renovating my apartment in Cape Town, I borrowed an adjoining closet space to add a shower to a half-bathroom. The shower wasn't deep—only 2 feet (600mm)—but it worked. The photo on the opposite page shows how a glass shower door makes the small space look bigger.

Photo by Wieland Gleich.

BEFORE: Powder Room with Hallway Closet

AFTER: Hallway Closet Converted into Shower

Photo by Wieland Gleich.

SHOWER IN A CLOSET

KITCHEN IN A CLOSET
Convert your kitchen into an extra room.

Get Rid of Your Kitchen

If you are not a gourmet cook—and especially if you live alone—you probably don't need a full kitchen. All you need is an empty closet. I suggest you assemble a kitchen inside that closet, one that suits your lifestyle. As a bonus, you may get yourself an extra room—your old kitchen!

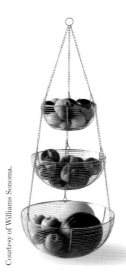

Courtesy of Williams Sonoma.

Live European-Style

Buy fresh. Buy only what you need and only when you need it. Hang a wire basket from the ceiling for fruits and vegetables. Position it so it doesn't touch the doors when they close.

Don't Stock Up

Let the supermarket do the stocking up for you. They have plenty of room. You don't. Just close your eyes whenever you see a "buy 1, get 1 free" sale.

Don't Forget Electric Plugs

You need at least four plugs for a microwave, refrigerator, toaster, and coffeemaker. Put them right above the appliance ledge.

Use Glass Shelves

Glass shelves let you see everything that's up there. They also look beautiful. Mine are 1" (25mm) thick and 8" (203mm) deep. Use adjustable metal strips and space them 8"–9" (203–229mm) apart near the bottom and 10"–12" (254–305mm) toward the top.

Divide the Shelves

Maximize your shelf space with gizmos like undershelf plate holders, under-shelf stemware holders, and shelf dividers. They come in wood, stainless steel, or plastic.

Add a Table on Wheels

A small table on wheels is a useful add-on when preparing a meal. And you can use it for serving later on.

Courtesy of Seville Classics.

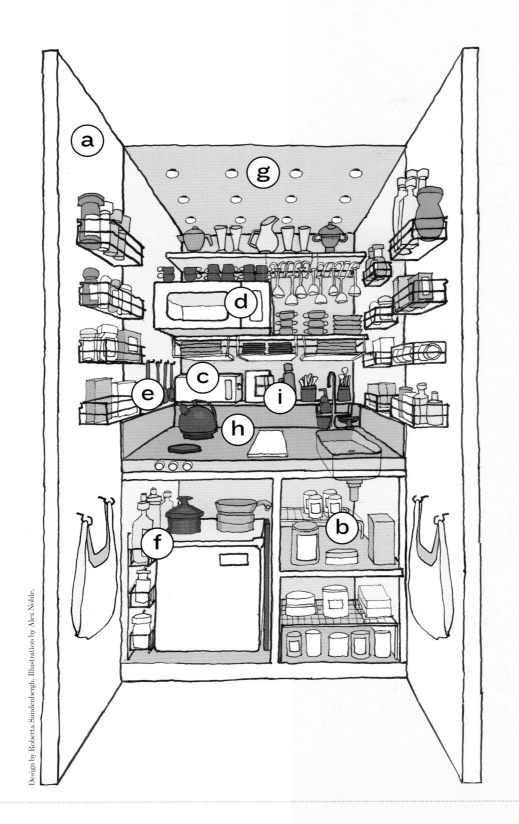

Design by Roberta Sandenbergh. Illustration by Alex Noble.

(b) Make a Pantry under the Sink

This space is far too precious to waste on just cleaning materials. Add one or two shelf dividers and make it into your food pantry. Use snap-tight plastic containers for loose groceries like oatmeal, rice, sugar, coffee, and tea.

(c) Find Small Appliances

Not very well advertised, but a small one-slice toaster is available online. As are many brands of small microwaves.

(d) Microwave

As the microwave is by far the most important item in your kitchen-closet, I hope nobody ever confirms the rumors of the harm it may be doing! The smallest one I could find was 18" (457mm) wide, 9" (229mm) high, and 12" (305mm) deep.

(e) Hang Up Utensils

Put up hooks for spatulas, spoons, strainers, scissors, and a can opener. But hang up only the bare essentials. If you find you don't use anything, give it away.

(f) Use Space around Refrigerator

I chose a bar-size model 24"x 24"x 24" (610mm x 610mm x 610mm) so I would have extra space on the top and sides of the fridge. I use the top for pots and pans. On one side, I stack trays. On the other side, I put up a shallow three-tier basket for cleaning materials.

(g) Add Drama

A wall mirror makes everything look bigger and more glamorous. So do ceiling lights that go on automatically when the doors open.

(h) Order a Custom Countertop

Order a custom-made stainless-steel countertop with a built-in sink. You can specify the exact size of your closet and a sink deep enough to avoid splashing. A good size for a small sink is 10" (254mm) wide, 12" (305mm) deep, and 8" (203mm) high. I suggest a bullnose front and a 6" backsplash.

(i) Order an Appliance Ledge

You can order a built-in back ledge together with your countertop. This is for raising appliances off the countertop to keep them from getting wet. Make it at least 6" (152mm) high and 4-1/2" (114mm) deep. Mine holds a toaster and a coffeemaker, plus a thermos flask and mugs to hold cutlery.

Courtesy of Acme Kitchenettes Corp.

Or a Larger Model

If you have a wider closet, there are larger mini-kitchens with ovens, microwaves, larger fridges, and dishwashers.

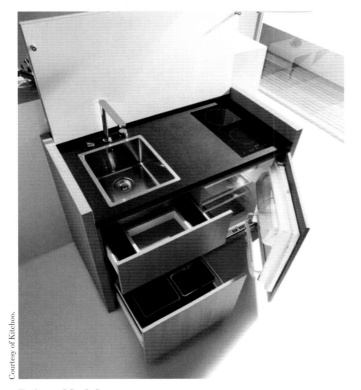

Courtesy of Kitchoo.

Deluxe Model

Buy a Standard Minikitchen

The simplest route is to start with a standard minikitchen like this one by Acme Kitchenettes in widths 36" (914mm), 39" (991mm), and 48" (1219mm). Most models come with a sink, undersink cabinet, bar fridge, and two burners. You rarely find one that exactly fits your closet, so be prepared to add a wood strip on at least one side.

Courtesy of Acme Kitchenettes Corp.

Extra Features

Or a More Stylish Model

If you intend to keep your mini-kitchen open to the living room, you can choose one that looks like a stylish cabinet. When the lid is closed, even the sink faucet disappears. In addition to a stainless steel sink and glass cooktop, there is also a tiny dishwasher.

KITCHEN IN A CLOSET

Decorative Doors for Closet-Kitchens

KITCHEN IN A CLOSET

MY STORY

In South Africa, I renovated a garage into a cottage for extra income to supplement my earnings as an architect. As part of the cottage's open-plan living room, I installed a minikitchen with a bar fridge and a two-burner cooktop. To close it off as a closet, I used tall skinny doors with decorative black-and-gold brass rubbings on the outside. These doors were the first things you saw when you came into the cottage. When I opened them up to reveal a kitchen behind, it was so unexpected that guests would step back and say, "Wow!"

CLOSED: Glass-Covered Brass Rubbings

OPEN: Shelves on Backs of Doors

Photos by Roberta Sandenbergh and D. ALLEN SA.

(a) Use Double Doors

Even skinny doors have plenty of room in back for wire basket-shelves, as seen on page 25. Use them for canned goods, jars, bottles, and spices.

CLOSED: Antique Wood Doors   **OPEN: Lights in Ceiling Turn On**

MY STORY, PART 2

In Manhattan—in the 500-square-foot studio apartment where I live today—it was a choice of having a closet-kitchen or no kitchen. My New York version is far more glamorous than the one in South Africa. It has a mirrored back wall, heavy glass shelves, small light bulbs in a metal ceiling, and carved mahogany doors. When the doors open, the lights in the ceiling go on and are reflected in the mirror. Once again, I open the doors to a chorus of "Wow!"

BED IN A CLOSET

Scale down a home's biggest space hog.

Take a Hint from U.S. Architect Buckminster Fuller

Buckminster Fuller once said, "Beds are empty 2/3 of the time—it's time we gave this some thought." Yes, a bed takes up an enormous amount of real estate and certainly doesn't deserve a 24-hour space.

Build a Murphy Bed into a Closet

You can also build a Murphy bed into any empty closet. For example, a queen-size bed will fit into a clear space 64" (1626mm) wide, 84" (2134mm) high, and 18" (457mm) deep.

Don't Be Afraid of the Word *Custom*

Whatever money you spend on custom work will be forgotten the minute you see the result: a Murphy bed that becomes an integral part of your apartment!

Keep It a Secret

The cleverness and secrecy are the fun parts of a Murphy bed. You don't have to tell.

Or Not So Secret

If you don't have visitors, just leave the bed down. When you put it up again, you may not even recognize your apartment. It will look enormous.

(a) Headboard, Curtain, and Valance

Add an upholstered headboard, a valance, and curtains in back of the bed. When the bed is down, these add-ons transform your closet into a bedroom.

(b) Side Shelves

Provide a place next to the bed for a shelf or a wall recess—even if it's only big enough for a bottle of water.

(c) Reading Lights

Use flat halogen fixtures or incandescent spots on the two sidewalls.

(d) Pillows, Blankets

Use a strap at the foot of the bed to secure pillows and extra blankets. Squash them in.

(e) Folding Doors

1. Use strong hinges to hold the doors open when the bed is down and to spread them out to separate the bed from the rest of the room. See Chapter 3: Divided Spaces.
2. Use magnets or hooks to keep doors shut when the bed is up.

Tips on Installing a Murphy Bed in a Closet:
1. Contact a certified Murphy bed installer to install the mechanism.
2. Hire a carpenter to build folding doors that fan out to become a partition.
3. Finish the doors so they blend in with the wall.

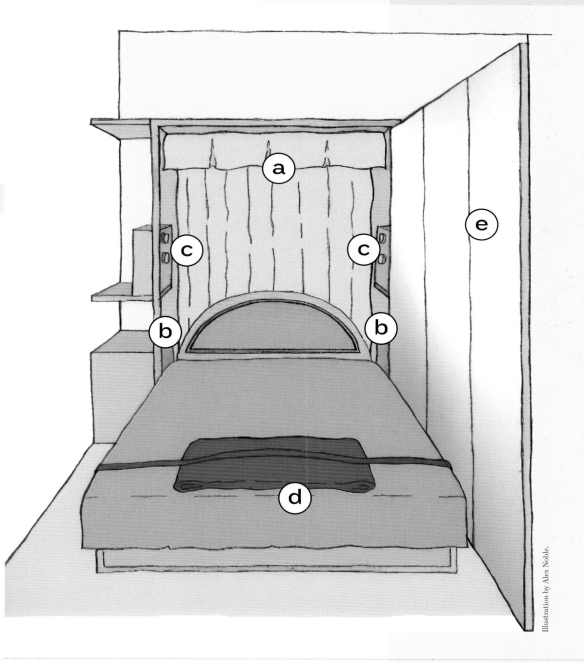

Illustration by Alex Noble.

Build In Mr. Murphy's magic tricks.

MY STORY

When I was lucky enough to find a studio with a view of Central Park, I wanted to see the view from every part of the apartment, especially the living area and the bed. So I installed a Murphy bed in a deep window recess right next to the view and had a carpenter close it off with folding doors that were covered with fabric on one side and mirrored on the other. When the bed is down, the doors fold out to become a room divider, and I can see the view from the bed. When the bed is up, the folding doors close, and I can see the view from the living area. Every year, I have a New Year's Eve party with fireworks at midnight and a buffet table in front of the folding doors. Only a few people "in the know" realize the doors are hiding a secret bedroom.

BEFORE: Bed Closed

AFTER: Bed Open

Photos by Adrian Wilson.

Hidden Bedroom in Living Room

Photo by Adrian Wilson.

OFFICE IN A CLOSET

Run an empire from your chair.

Today's teeny electronic gadgets cry out to live inside a closet. It's the perfect size. Who needs a big space for a tablet or a laptop?

As a Space Definer
The enclosed space of a closet defines your workspace and gives you the psychological feeling of being in a real office.

As the Tidy Police
Working in a closet means you have to keep putting things away—over and over again. Perhaps more than anywhere else in your home, you need a dedicated spot here for everything you use.

As a Life Divider
An office-closet is not just a space saver. It's a life divider. Working from home can be confusing. This keeps it straight. When you're finished with work, close the doors, and your office disappears. All your files, papers, and office worries are out of sight. Lock the doors, and it's time for your other life. You've gone home, even if you are already home.

(a) Double Doors
Skinny double doors provide privacy when they're open. They make you feel you're in a separate room, instead of hanging out in a corridor.

(b) Use the Backs of Doors
Put up wire basket-shelves. Find a "hold-all" that looks like a shoe bag on steroids.

(c) Hang Up Trash
Use a plastic bag from the supermarket.

(d) Custom Desktop
I suggest 3/4" (19mm) plywood with a front edging. Add a molding so things don't fall down. Standard desks are 29" (737mm) high, but mine is 26-1/2" (673mm) because I'm short. Keep your desktop clear. It's the only way to live in a closet.

(e) Install Back Ledge
Mine is 7" (178mm) high, 8" (203mm) deep—mainly for my phone, pens, and coffee mug. I slide my laptop underneath, to make room for the jobs that don't require a computer.

(f) Shelf above Desk
No more than 18" (457mm) above your desk, so you can reach it without getting up. Only for the most current "IN" stuff.

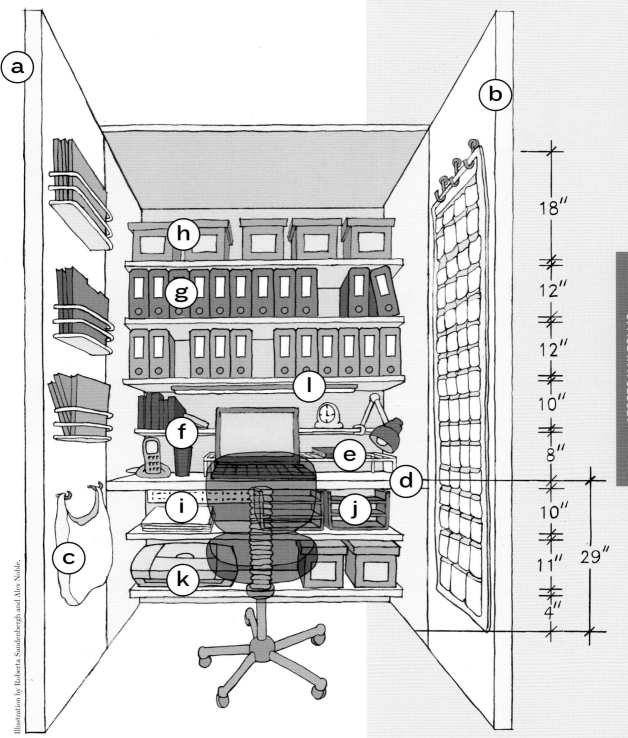

Illustration by Roberta Sandenbergh and Alex Noble.

18″
12″
12″
10″
8″
10″
11″
4″

29″

(g) Magazine File Boxes

Use magazine file boxes with cutouts in back that you can tilt downward from a seated position. These files are for anything that is PENDING or WORTH SAVING. Prune the contents carefully. Throw away anything you can find online. Label them alphabetically.

(h) Use Top Shelf

This is for archive boxes. Keep all your archives in one place, even old tax forms. When you start putting things in separate places, you forget about them.

(i) Electric Plugs

Don't underestimate how many you need. I have three lights, a cell phone, an iPad, a laptop, a hard drive, an all-in-one printer, a router, and a modem! Buy a grommet and cut a 2"-diameter (51mm) hole in your desktop for your wires. Label both ends of every wire!

(j) Underdesk Supply Shelf

For anything that doesn't fit on the backs of the doors: paper, envelopes, ink cartridges, three-hole punches, paper shredders.

(k) Bottom Shelf

My choice for the printer! I just lean to one side and bend slightly. My theory is that once I sit down, I stay put for as long as possible.

(l) Lights

Lighting makes a small space bigger. For general light, buy the longest under-shelf fluorescent fixture you can find. To avoid glare, put up a wood fascia like a kitchen cabinet. For direct light, I suggest a folding lamp like the Ottlite or the space-saving accessory lamp show here. When you sit down and turn on your light in the morning, it marks the start of a new workday!

MY STORY

There was no room for an architectural studio in our small Greenwich Village apartment, so we used the kitchen, which was large for a Manhattan apartment. It had a refrigerator, a sink cabinet, and a stove, all in a single line along one wall. We put our drawing boards against the opposite wall with a small pullout table underneath. To separate the studio from the kitchen, we installed a curtain on a sliding track on the ceiling. All our office stuff like an electric typewriter, paper, and supplies went into the pantry closet. Now, if only we had a computer with CAD software, we could have thrown away the electric typewriter and the bulky drawing boards and fit everything in the closet. But that was the 1960s. Back then, who knew?

KID IN A CLOSET

Make a cozy hideaway for a child.

Children love to hide away in secret places with their favorite book. If you want to make reading a secret pleasure for your child, I suggest finding a place to create a reading nook.

Find a Closet You Rarely Use

It could be an underused hall closet, a linen closet, or even a closet in a master bedroom. If you can clear out some stuff, trade it in for a happy child.

DIY

- Take the door off a closet
- Paint the walls a bright color
- Fit out the floor with cushions
- Add wall bookshelves
- Let the magic begin!

Illustration by Hafiz Omer Shafiq.

Create a Reading Nook

EAT-WORK-SLEEP IN A CLOSET

Make a meal out of nothing.

Some Tricks from Chinese Architects B.L.U.E. Studio.

The B.L.U.E. Studio architects used a closet-sized space to create a cozy dining nook and a place to work—and then topped it off by converting it into a space for two beds. There is a single bed that pulls out from below, some bookshelves on the side, and a pulley system that drops down a second bed from the ceiling.

EAT   **WORK**

How You Can Apply These Ideas

You may not want to eat, sleep, and work in such a tiny space. But you can probably find plenty of opportunities to stack functions tightly when you are short of space. Storage and sleeping can easily fit over working and eating, even when they are not fitted into a closet.

Ventilation

It is best to choose an area with a window for tightly packed spaces. Without a window, you will need mechanical ventilation. Small areas have to be able to breathe.

Photos courtesy of B.L.U.E. Studio.

SLEEP

WARDROBE ALL-IN-ONE CLOSET
Hang up only what you are proud to wear.

Use Only One Closet
I believe everyone—except royalty and celebrities—can fit their current wardrobe into a single closet. That is, if you hang up only what fits you, looks good on you, and is appropriate to your current lifestyle. Everything else should be stored or given away.

Choose Carefully What You Hang Up
The refrain "I have a closet full of clothes, but nothing to wear" is true for most of us. Sometimes we have clothes packed in so tight it's hard to pull anything out. No wonder it takes us forever to get dressed. So hang up only what you love to put on. Only these items qualify for one-closet status.

Get Rejects off Their Hangers
Instead of taking up room in a high-rent closet, rejects that you can't bear to give away can reside on a low-rent shelf or under a bed. Pack them into boxes, bags, or suitcases. Label them in big letters: *Thin clothes, Fat clothes, Out-of-Season, Out-of-Style*. Better still: give them away.

Consolidate and Compact
When you are absolutely sure everything in your one closet is what you need and love, then you can start consolidating and compacting your wardrobe into a minimum of space.

Make Everything Visible
Beware of putting anything in an unmarked box or drawer—or, even worse, a storeroom. It is as good as throwing it out. You will forget that you ever owned it.

Make Everything Vertical
To save space, think *multihanger*. Everything should hang down vertically from the clothes rod. I suggest using multiple hangers like Wonder Platinum hangers.

Make Life Simple
You can look forward to a much simpler life. Picture it. You have to get ready to go out. You open your closet door and see at a glance all the things you love to wear. They are all clean and pressed. You just have to listen to the weather forecast. In a matter of minutes, you are ready to go.

Make It Personal
Decorate your closet. Make it your own. Put up art posters—even on the ceiling.

Keep It under Review
Seasons change. Styles change. You change. Reevaluate. Evict what you don't wear. Rents are too high for non-performers. If you are unsure about an item, pack it away for further review. After a while, it may start looking good again. Who knows? It may even graduate to one-closet status.

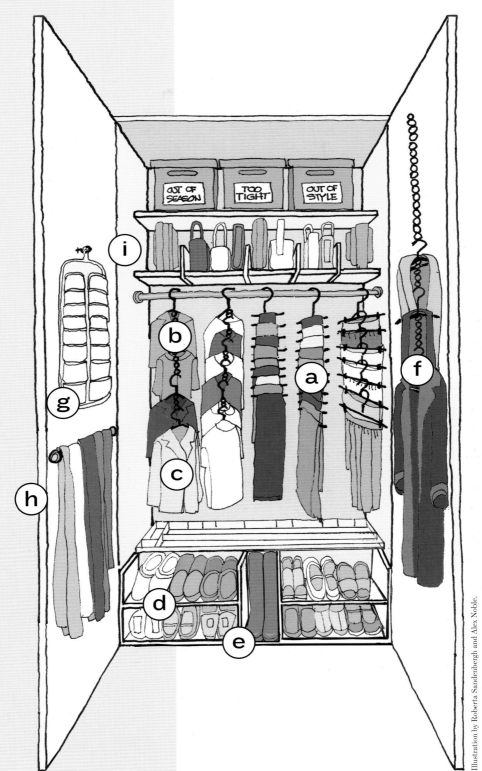

OUT OF SEASON

TOO TIGHT

OUT OF STYLE

i

b

a

f

g

c

h

d

e

(a) Use Multiclip Hangers

Use hangers that come with little clips for skirts and pants with hooks in front to link six to eight items in a vertical row. You can pull them off at the bottom without disturbing the others on top.

(b) Use Interlinked Hangers

Use multiple hangers like Wonder Platnum for blouses and jackets. Garments go all the way down in a linked chain. You can get five items in a line.

(c) Separate by Type and Color

Jackets should live with jackets, blouses with blouses, and lines of hangers with their own color schemes. Black-gray. Tan-white. Green-blue-purple. Red-orange-yellow. When they're separated by type and color, things are very easy to find. It also looks great. Stand back and admire.

(d) Put Shoes on The Floor

You can fit at least 2 double-decker shoe racks on the floor of an average closet. This equals a total of 12 pairs of shoes—probably far fewer than you have right now. Get rid of the shoes that don't deserve to be there. Do you really need 3 pairs of sneakers? Trust me, 12 pairs of shoes will be all you need if you keep them all polished and well heeled in a pared-down one-closet wardrobe.

(e) Squeeze Boots In

Use "boot tongs" to keep boots upright. Squeeze them into whatever floor space is left in between the shoe racks, or in between the shoe rack and the wall. These are available from Bed Bath and Beyond.

(f) Put Coats on The Backs of Doors

Hang coats on hooks on the inside of the closet door. For heavy coats, use a garage wall hanger.

(g) Hang Up Your Jewelry

Jewelry boxes are too difficult. I like the hanging see-through bags with a gazillion little pockets. Hang it on the inside of the closet door. It will lift your spirits every time you open up the door.

(h) Hang Up Your Scarves

I suggest installing a swinging wood rack on the back of a door or in the corner of a wall. The one shown below is from Hammacher Schlemmer and comes in 5 and 10-rod sizes. It is meant for trousers, but I think it is even better for hanging up scarves. This is an example of what I call "visible storage," things that don't have to be shut away in a drawer or a closet but can hide in plain sight for everyday enjoyment.

Photo by Adrian Wilson.

Put Handbags on Shelf

I find hanging bag gizmos take up too much room. I prefer vertical dividers on a shelf. On a 42" (1067mm) shelf, I managed to fit two backpacks, two computer cases, and six handbags.

Put Scarves on Hooks

This is for your everyday scarves, the ones you throw on just as you leave the house. Keep them handy and divide them by colors. I have a hook for white-tan scarves, one for blue-greens, two for orange-reds, and two for black-browns.

Photography by Akihisa Ueno, KonMari Media, Inc., Marie Kondo, https://konmari.com

Fold Vertically in Drawers

You've probably been folding clothes the wrong way for years. Learn to fold pants, tops, sweaters, and underwear into neat rectangles and stack them vertically in drawers. You can see everything at a glance, and it all stays in place (from Marie Kondo's *The Life-Changing Joy of Tidying Up*).

MY STORY

An older European woman named Yolanda worked as a draftswoman in my first architectural office. She dressed in very sophisticated and perfectly coordinated outfits, while I was still wearing sweaters and skirts left over from my college days. (Incredibly, women were not allowed to wear pants in those days.) Yolanda assumed the role of personal advisor and helped me choose clothes that she thought suitable for a professional woman. She inspected me every day when I arrived at work. Everything coordinated. No stains. No creases. Perfect! She would say to me, "Keep in your closet only what you are proud to wear." Over the many years since then, whenever I find myself accumulating clothes that I don't really love and am not proud to wear, I think of her words and start stuffing the unloved items into big black bags to give away. Her words have become my philosophy for all aspects of my life: if you don't love it, get rid of it.

CORNER SPACES

A corner is almost an extra room.

Corners are COZY.
We are corner dwellers by instinct. We may like to look at open spaces, but we choose to live in corners. Where do you like to sit in a restaurant? First choice: in a corner. Second choice: against a wall. The tables in the middle sometimes remain empty until every other seat is taken.

Corners are SECURE.
In a corner, you have a wall on either side of you; nobody can sneak up from behind. This gives you a feeling of control. You can look out at the scene and think: "I'm all right here. I can see everyone. Nobody can get at me."

Corners are for LIVING.
When you are planning your living room, a good rule is to keep the open areas for show and the corners for living. A big room with "floating island" seating is a good thing for impressing your guests. But for everyday usefulness, a corner wins out every time. It's the best place to read a book, watch TV, or have a drink with a friend.

Corners are for the first choice for Everything and Everywhere:
- Corners make the most popular **PUBS**.
- Corners make the most efficient **KITCHENS**.
- Corners make the most private **WORKING** spaces.
- Corners make the coziest **BEDROOMS**.

When planning your living space, **look first at the corners!**

KITCHEN IN A CORNER

Cut a notch out of your living room.

(a) Build a Low Wall

A 48" (1219mm)-high wall can separate the kitchen from the rest of the room and also serve as a place to put down a tray or a glass of wine.

(b) Buy a Minikitchen

Standard models usually come in widths 39" (991mm), 42" (1067mm), and 48" (1219mm), with a refrigerator, cooktop, and sink. See Chapter 1: Closet Spaces.

(c) Add a Shelf for a Microwave Oven

Put a microwave shelf at the same height as the top of the partition. Make sure it's easy to reach.

(d) Use Top of Microwave

Don't waste the space on top. For my South African teatimes, I used it for a tea tray complete with cups, saucers, teaspoons, sugar, creamer, and teapot.

(e) Build Ledge for Appliances

Make it 6" (152mm) above the mini-kitchen, to keep appliances from getting wet.

(f) Add Shelves below Ledge

These are handy for pots and pans.

(g) Make a Side Partition

A partition at the other side of the minikitchen can be used for hanging up utensils.

(h) Hang a Wire Basket

A basket from the ceiling is a handy and decorative way to keep produce fresh and aerated.

Photo by D. ALLEN SA.

MY STORY

When I decided to divide my house in South Africa into two separate cottages for extra income, I used the original kitchen as a bedroom and installed a minikitchen in a corner of the living room. There was no oven—or even a toaster-oven—so I made do with a microwave oven and an electric kettle. It was a marvelously efficient kitchen and a lot of fun to use.

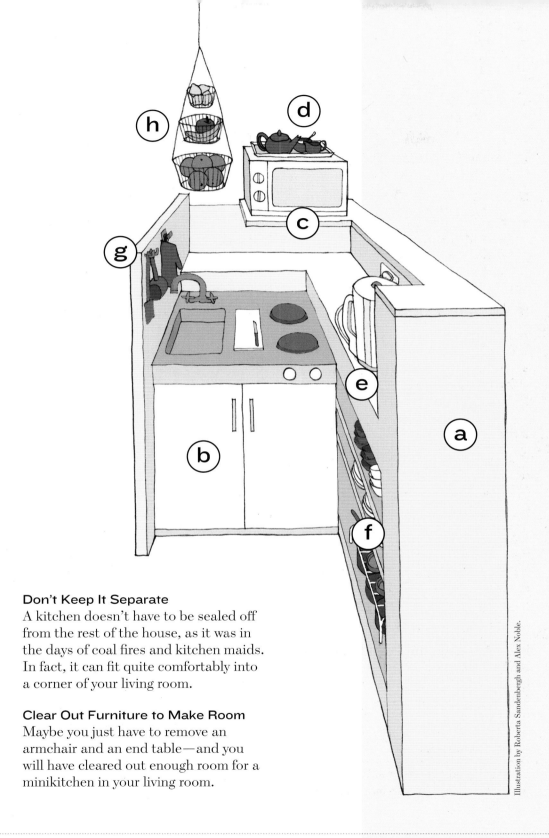

Illustration by Roberta Sandenbergh and Alex Noble.

Don't Keep It Separate
A kitchen doesn't have to be sealed off from the rest of the house, as it was in the days of coal fires and kitchen maids. In fact, it can fit quite comfortably into a corner of your living room.

Clear Out Furniture to Make Room
Maybe you just have to remove an armchair and an end table—and you will have cleared out enough room for a minikitchen in your living room.

DINING IN A CORNER

Make every meal cozy.

Build in a Two-sided Bench or Use a Ready-made.
Any small table and chairs will fit nicely into a corner.

Make It Seem like a Separate Space
Paint the corner walls a contrasting color from the rest of the room.

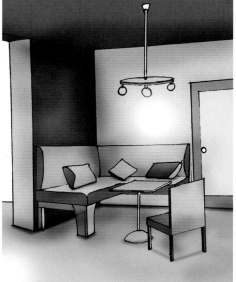

Illustration by Hafiz Omar Shafiq.

Design by Alyssa Kapito Interiors.

Finding a comfortable place to sit down and eat can be a difficult task in a small apartment. But you can usually find a small corner. It may have a plant or chair or piece of sculpture hogging the space. Just move it away.

Your dining corner can even be right next to the front door of your apartment, like the one shown here.

You may have to find a handy husband or handyman to make it fit exactly into your space, but you will be thanking him for many years afterward. A corner is always the coziest place in the room.

DINING IN A CORNER

BATHROOM MADE OF CORNERS

Give every fixture a private nook.

Use the Corners to Save Space
If you are building or renovating a bathroom, consider using only the corners of the bathroom to install your fixtures. It will be the most efficient use of the available space.

Make a Shower Corner
Fit the shower into a corner of its own, ideally with a curved glass partition.

Tuck In the Toilet and Sink
Fit the toilet and sink basin into separate corners.

Maximize the Space
The use of corners for the bath fixtures will automatically maximize the space in the bathroom by leaving the center free for moving around.

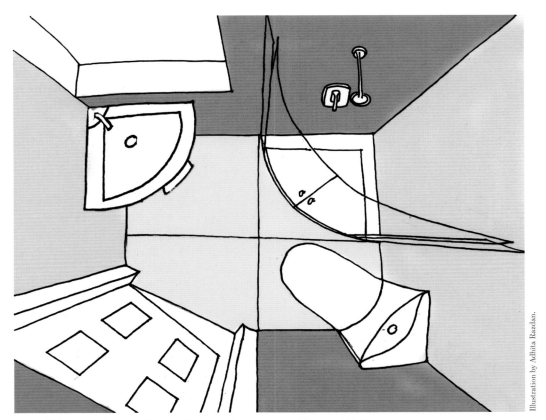

Illustration by Adhita Razdan.

Aerial View of Corner Basin, Corner Shower, and Corner Toilet

BATHTUB IN A CORNER
Create a tranquil refuge.

Buy a Corner Acrylic Tub

Consider a ready-made acrylic bathtub for a corner of your bathroom. A standard size is 48" (1219mm) by 48" (1219mm). They come curved or five-sided with two sides touching the walls.

Courtesy of Aquatica Plumbing Group Inc.

Or a Walk-in Corner Bathtub

This is an excellent solution for the elderly or handicapped because you can take a bath without having to climb over the side of a tub. You can even convert an existing bathtub into a walk-in model. They are smaller than normal bathtubs and come in many styles.

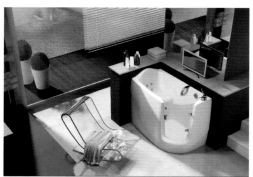

Courtesy of Gruppo Tres.

(a) Add a Seat and Ledges

A seat and ledges on all the sides will make a small bathtub seem like a luxurious spa.

(b) Use Small Ceramic Tiles

Very small tiles on the walls, ledge, step, seat, and tub make everything look bigger.

(c) Surround It with Mirrors

Mirrors create the illusion that there is another bathtub on the other side of the wall.

MY STORY

My house in South Africa had only one bathroom. When I divided it into two separate cottages, I had to find room for a second one. There was a small space that had been a breakfast nook. This was just enough room for a tiny bathroom with a toilet and a sink, but I wanted a bathtub, as well. For this I had to borrow a corner of the living room behind the bathroom door. By digging down two steps, the top of a sunken tub came level with the floor. You had to enter the tub from its far end, but this ultratiny corner hidden behind the door became my secret refuge. In the calming warm water of the little tub, I was able to find long periods of peace and tranquillity.

Create a Custom Sunken Tub
Add to your list when renovating your bathroom.

Photo by D. Allen SA.

HOME OFFICE IN A CORNER

Enjoy your underused living room.

Make It Compact
A desk in a corner—compact and self-contained—allows you to have everything at arm's length.

Find Peace and Privacy
Working in a corner gives you privacy from the rest of the room. It feels peaceful to have your own little nook.

Use a Ready-made Solution
This design is a clever minimalist solution by misosoupdesign.com, using a single strip of laminated wood that curves around to create a place to store books as well as a place to work.

Or DIY
You can adapt this stripped-down idea without using curved strips of laminated wood. Just install a small desk with connected overhead shelves. The problem will be to keep this open design neat and tidy.

Courtesy of Miso Soup Design.

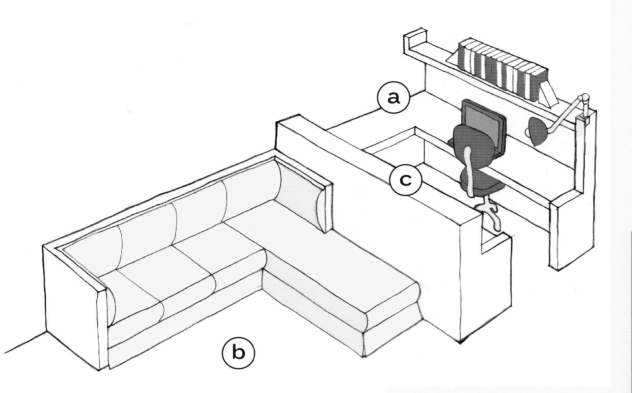

(a) Compact Corner

A desk built into a corner—compact and self-contained—allows you to have everything at arm's length.

(b) Room to Walk Around

Because your work area is so compact, it leaves plenty of room to walk around the rest of the room. Get up and stretch your legs or talk to your guests—away from your pile of private papers.

(c) Privacy

For privacy, add shelves on top of your desk or put a screen in front.

Use Your Best Room

Your home is your castle, and, if you work at home, you may as well sit near the throne. Instead of hiding away in a bedroom, why not carve out a place for yourself in a corner of your usually deserted living room?

Dress Up

To feel as if you're in a real office, start dressing up for work.

Add Some Privacy

For privacy, add a partition or open shelves in front of your desk.

HOME OFFICE IN A CORNER

Illustration by Hafiz Omer Shafiq.

MY STORY

My house in South Africa had a curved entryway between the living area and the bedrooms. When I divided the house into two separate cottages, one to live in and one to rent out, the old entry hall became my studio. The corner between the two cottages was a very cozy place to work, and the old front stable door became the private entrance. With the top half of the door left open, the space was always full of air and bright sunlight.

When I made the switch from hand drawing to CAD (computer-aided design), it worked even better. I could throw away my bulky drawing board with its now-obsolete slide rule. I could throw out my huge drawing cabinets. And even the "Sweet's Catalogs" became a thing of the past.

Photos by D. Allen SA.

Add Shelves and Drawers

Use every inch of your corner— with drawers on either side of your chair, overhead books, and a wall for calendars, reminders, and uplifting quotations.

Use a Window

A window will give you natural light and raise your spirits, especially when your work isn't going well. It's always nice to take a peek at what's going on outside. And a window recess can add a few inches of extra desk space. In an old building with very thick walls, this could be a foot (305mm) or more.

Put Up A Swing-Lamp

A wall-mounted swing-arm lamp fixture saves space on the desktop and provides maximum light.

BABY IN A CORNER

Borrow part of a room.

If you don't have an extra room or an empty closet, use the corner of a room for a new baby. You can even choose one close to your bed. You will sleep more relaxed hearing the baby breathing and knowing you have put off—at least for a while—the decision to move.

(a) Install a Crib Rail

For the open side of the "crib," attach a wood rail to the wall with a strong catch. Or, as in Chapter 1: Closet Spaces (see page 13), use a metal rail meant for toddler beds. Just attach it very securely to the board underneath the mattress.

(b) Buy a Changing Table

A small chest of drawers at the side of the crib is all you need. (Ikea has one.) Use a plastic-covered pad on top. Use the drawers for diapers and baby wipes.

(c) Use a Cabinet as Support

This will support the crib and also provide storage. In Chapter 1: Baby in A Closet (see page 14), I suggested using deep file drawers. A sliding door cabinet will work, as well. If it is a shallow drawer, it will require a deep board on top to support the mattress.

(d) Make a "Crib"

The corner walls form two sides of the "crib." Your chest of drawers-cum-changing table will be the third. All you have to buy is a crib mattress and a three-sided crib "bumper" (fabric-covered pieces of foam with holes in them).

(e) Add a Valance

Just for fun, put a ruffled valance above the baby corner. Install a track in the ceiling or a rod on the wall. It gives the corner an identity and lifts your spirits when you look at it.

(f) Get a Screen with Pockets

You can buy ready-made screens, hinged together and fitted with storage pockets. Or enlist a handyman or a handy husband to make them. Cover the panels with padded fabric and sew on different-size pockets to hold all the baby stuff like talcum powder and baby lotion.

Courtesy of Pocketz Folding Screens.

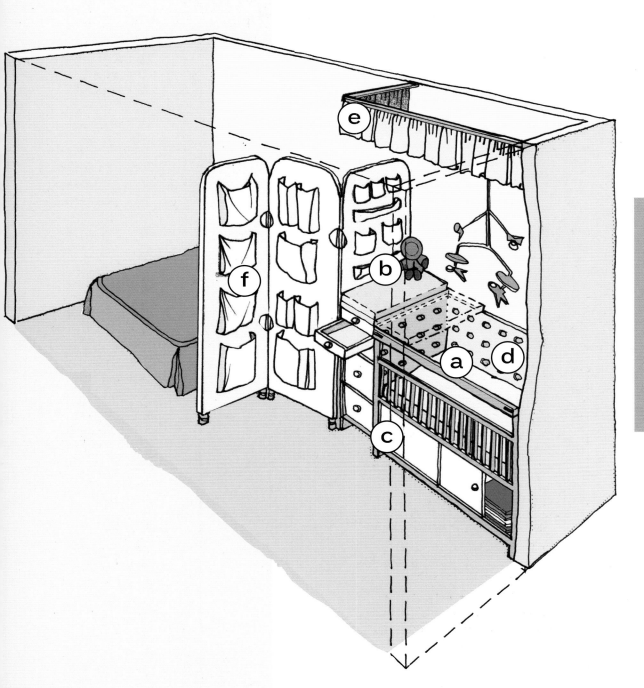

KID IN A CORNER

Create a space to read.

Use Any Room

A kid's reading corner can be in any room of the house: the living room, the entry area, the hallway, or even the kitchen. This is a simple way to give your children a private place to read without having to empty out a closet. (See Chapter 1, Closet Spaces, page 13.)

Don't Make It Lonely

The corner should not be tucked away in a lonely bedroom. It should be where the rest of the family hangs out—where everything is going on.

Decorate the Walls

Once you have cleared out a suitable corner, have fun with it. Paint it a contrasting color—or more than one color—to make it stand out from the rest of the room.

Cushion the Floor

Put down a carpet—or even a leftover piece of wall-to-wall carpeting.

Make Comfortable Seats

Plump down beanbags or cushions on the floor and pile them up to make them really comfy.

Be Careful of Headroom

Normal-depth bookshelves have to be put up high enough so kids won't bump their heads when they stand up. But the shelves also can't be so high that the kids can't reach the books.

Put Up Spice Racks as Bookshelves

The racks meant for spices are not very deep, so kids won't bump their heads on them, and they make perfect bookracks for kid–size books. The front part of the rack holds the books firmly in place, and wood racks will look great in your living room.

KID IN A CORNER

BED IN A CORNER

Curl up and feel secure.

Make It Cozy

A bed in the middle of a room may be better for bed making, but it doesn't feel as cozy or secure as one in a corner. There's nothing like curling up in a bed in a corner. You just have to stretch to put on the sheets.

Leave Room for Other Activities

A bed in the middle of a room often leaves no more than a narrow corridor between your bed and the wall. A bed in a corner frees the rest of the room for activities like exercising, dressing, or sewing.

Use an Attic Loft

To the right, you see the sleeping loft that I converted from a kitchen attic in my thatch-roof house in South Africa. The bed is built into the pointy corner of the roof, so close to the thatch that I had to put up a mosquito net to keep away the insects that lived there!

Make a Corner into a Bedroom

On the page opposite, you see a left-over corner that I converted into a small bedroom in my Cape Town apartment. All I needed was enough room for a passage at the side of the bed.

MY STORY

Wherever I lived—in New York or South Africa; alone or with a partner—I have always chosen to sleep in a corner. Not only do corner beds take up less space, but they always seem a safer and happier place in which to close your eyes and dream.

Perhaps my preference for sleeping in a corner came from the lovely weekends I used to spend many years ago with my husband, John, in the V-shaped bow of a 26' (7.9m) Erikson sailboat on Long Island Sound.

Photo by D. Allen SA.

Photo by Wieland Gleich.

APARTMENT IN A CORNER

Live, sleep, dine in a single space.

Create the Ultimate Corner

This studio apartment in the Netherlands, designed by Queeste Architects, is my ideal example of fitting everything into one compact corner: living, dining, and sleeping. It uses a sofa that encompasses a queen-size bed and curls around a small dining table.

How to Adapt This Idea

Anyone who lives in a single room is a good candidate for this unusual idea. You can turn a cramped living space into a spacious apartment simply by condensing all your living functions. Tucking everything into a corner of a room frees up the rest of the space.

Choose a Corner

If possible, choose a corner of the room that is opposite a window. It must be as far away from the kitchen, bathroom, and closets as possible.

Think of It like a Jigsaw Puzzle

First, measure the corner and draw it as a plan on a piece of paper. Then, as you find pieces of furniture to fit into the corner, draw their footprints on colored paper and glue them to the plan. Your goal is to get all the different pieces to fit together perfectly.

Find Sofa Sections

Go online and type in sofa sections. Try to find standard pieces with a round section at one end. If you can't find the exact sizes you need, look for manufacturers that offer custom services. Remember that space is money and you want it to fit perfectly.

Fit In a Queen-Size Bed

Buy a queen-size bed and drop it into the open space in the middle of the sofa sections. Leave a few inches of space around the bed. Then, raise the bed so that the mattress is just above the level of the sofa.

Make a Bed Cover to Match the Sofa

What you need is a mattress cover in the same fabric as the sofa that can be slipped easily over the sheets and blankets, no matter how rumpled.

Cover the Bed Pillows

Pillow covers that are made of the same fabric as the sofa must be large enough for the bed pillows to be slipped in and out easily.

Buy a Small Round Table

What you want for this space is the smallest-diameter table on the market with a slim pedestal base.

Add a False Ceiling

If you want to go the extra mile to recreate the wonderful coziness of this design, you can add a partially angled false ceiling painted white to reflect the light of the window opposite the sofa.

Paint the Walls White

White walls will add to a feeling of spaciousness.

Photos courtesy of MAFF Apartments The Hague, www.maff.nl. Design by Queeste Architects.

APARTMENT IN A CORNER

VILLAGE MADE OF CORNERS

Use angles to create privacy.

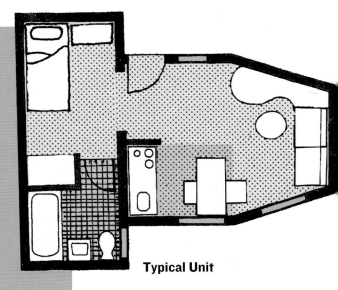

Typical Unit

MY STORY

This was my first architectural job in South Africa, a retirement community in the suburbs of Johannesburg. When I read the brief that said each unit could be no more than 43 square meters (463 square feet), I saw that they were just like studio apartments in Manhattan! This development was built under apartheid: for whites only. But when I came back 25 years later, I was heartened to see people of all colors walking up and down the steps of my little village. I felt especially happy to see that the stable doors were helping to bring the residents closer to their neighbors by allowing them to chat through the open "windows."

Corner Angles for Privacy

The corner angles ensure each unit's privacy, so no two face in the same direction.

Corner Bed Spaces

I borrowed the area next to the bathroom for a 5' (1.52m)-wide bed space. This can accommodate a queen-size mattress accessed from the foot of the bed or a single bed from the side.

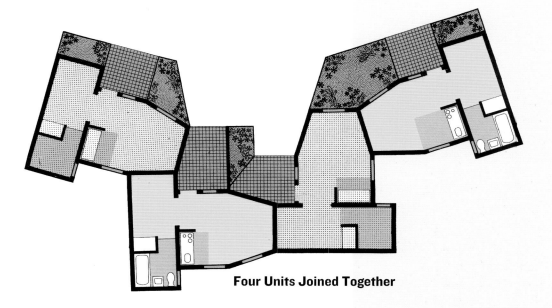

Illustrations by Roberta Sandenbergh.

Four Units Joined Together

Corner Entry Gardens

The entry areas were designed as small gardens to separate one unit from another. Low-rise multiunit developments can all use this idea.

Stable Doors

A stable door, or a door that opens in two sections—one at the top, one at the bottom—allows a door to act as an open window when the top is left open. This idea made for better neighbors and fewer lonely people in the community.

Illustration by Bill Birrer.

Mini-village.

3

DIVIDED SPACES

Get two for the space of one.

Dividers Provide Privacy

If you live with anyone other than yourself, you may want to be able to sit at your desk or lie down in your bed without anyone else barging in. Dividers provide a barrier between you and the rest of the world.

Dividers Define and Hide

When you enter a room and cannot see everything at once, a screen adds an air of mystery. It can seem like a much larger room or even several rooms, when you can see only one small section at a time.

A Divider Can Be Anything

A space partition can be as simple as hanging up a curtain—or as complicated as building a sliding wall. It all depends on your needs and your budget. There are countless materials you can use to make a partition.

In this chapter, I discuss these ideas:
- *Bookcase*
- *Curtains*
- *Folding screens*
- *Folding screens with built-in chairs*
- *Folding screens with built-in shelves*
- *Sliding screens*
- *Roller blinds*
- *Zigzag walls*
- *U-shaped walls*
- *Sliding walls*
- *Metal rods*

BOOKCASE PARTITION

Gain a double function.

Think Perpendicular
Plunk down a bookcase perpendicular to a wall, and—presto—you have a divided space. It doesn't have to reach the ceiling, but the higher the better for the illusion of a separate room.

Use All the Sides
One side of a bookcase can be for dining, the other for sleeping, and an in-between space for a living-room sofa.

Add Storage Space
Fill the shelves with your favorite books or decorative items.

Create a psychological division.

No Physical Barrier
You may not have to add a thing in order to divide a room. Just turn around a piece of furniture.

Move a Sofa
Place a sofa at the foot of your bed so your back faces the sleeping area. Or put a table at the back of a sofa, so it forms a countertop for a dining area.

Add a Headboard
Just a tall headboard can separate and provide privacy for a sleeping area.

Add a Tall Plant
Does a plant count as a piece of furniture? Maybe not—but you get the idea. A tall plant may be all you need to provide the illusion of a separate space.

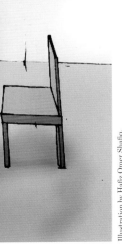

Illustration by Hafiz Omer Shafiq.

BOOKCASE PARTITION

CURTAIN PARTITION

Find an extra bedroom.

Cut Down a Too-Long Space

In this example—a one-bedroom apartment in Cape Town, South Africa—I started with a living room that was 11' (3m) wide and 19' (6m) long, a bit too long for its width, but similar to many studio apartments in New York. I cut off the end of this "too-long" living room and installed a curtain as a divider in order to get a second bedroom.

Don't Cut Off Too Much

You only have to cut off a little more than the length of the bed if you put the bed against the far wall. My new space was 6-1/2 feet (2m) long. Access to the bed was from the two sides.

Scale Down Living-Room Furniture

Your new living room after a partition will be smaller but cozier. The closer to a square, the better for conversation. I bought small-scale furniture consisting of two 48" (1219mm) settees and one 36" (914mm)-diameter round dining table.

Look for Dividing Opportunities

Any overlong or overwide room, or a room with an alcove, can be used effectively to cut off a space in order to gain an extra room in your home. Some tips:

(a)
Position the Bed Carefully

Place the head of the bed against the far wall and hang the curtain at the foot. Allow at least 18" (457mm) at each side of the bed and use fitted sheets and a duvet to allow for easy bed making.

(b)
Double Up the Curtain

Use a two-sided curtain, so you can see the fabric pattern from both sides and get better sound insulation.

(c)
Curtain the Side Walls

Hang lightweight floor-to-ceiling curtains on the walls around the bed for a cozy Arabian Nights feeling.

(d)
Add a Desk or Closet

If you want a desk at one side of the new space, you can allow as little as 24" (610mm) for a narrow desk with a folding chair. You could also add a sliding door closet. (For fun, use mirrored doors.)

(e)
Install a Light Switch

To make your new space seem like a real bedroom, install a separate switch for the bed lamps or ceiling light.

(f)
Provide Ventilation

Make sure there's a window, fan or air conditioner. In my case, the room already had a high window at the far end.

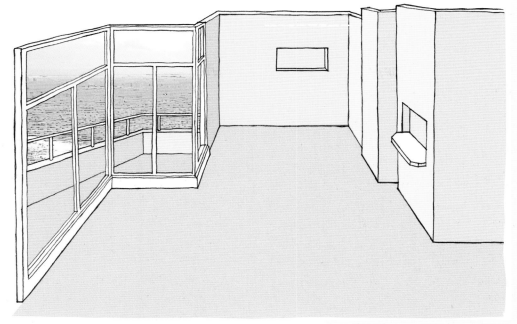

BEFORE: Long Narrow Living Room

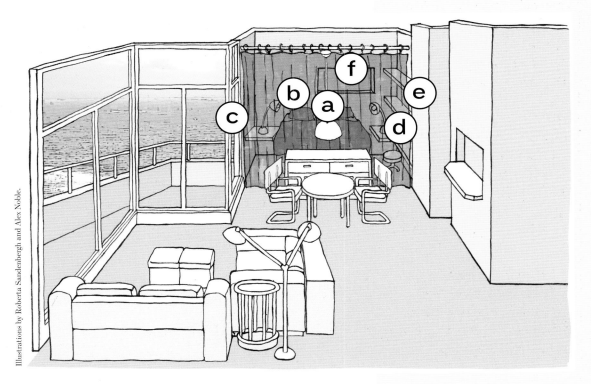

Illustrations by Roberta Sandenbergh and Alex Noble.

AFTER: Extra Bedroom

Photo by Roberta Sandenbergh.

MY STORY

I found this beach apartment when my American friend Arthur took a trip with me around South Africa. When we got down to Cape Town, he took one look at the gorgeous white sands of Clifton beach and said, "This is where I want to spend the rest of my life." He decided to cancel our safari at Kruger Park and visit a real estate agent instead. The agent showed us an apartment right on the beach, with a lovely view of the Twelve Apostles Mountain Range. For me, it was love at first sight. It was only 650 square feet (60m²) and had only one bedroom, but I knew I could find more space in the apartment. So I bought it without consulting Arthur, who still insisted it was too small. I spent almost six months renovating the flat: without a car, without a telephone, and without the Internet (it was 1994). When Arthur came to visit me six months later, he asked in amazement, "Are you sure this is the same apartment?"

FOLDOUT MURPHY BED DOORS

Fan out to divide a room.

Close the Doors When Bed Is Up
Use four narrow doors attached with piano hinges inside a Murphy bed frame. Attach them to the frame with heavy-duty hinges on one side only.

Open the Doors with Bed Down
When you pull the panels open, they fan out to become a room divider.

Gain Flexible Space
This is a clever way to partition a space and then unpartition it, by folding a screen flat against a wall when not in use.

Hinge the Screen from the Wall
Attach a folding screen to a wall with heavy-duty hinges. When closed, use a hook or a magnet to keep them flat against the wall.

Keep It Off the Floor
When you attach a folding screen to the wall, raise it above the baseboard to keep the floor clear for cleaning.

Make It Blend In
Finish your folding screens to match the adjacent walls with paint, fabric, or wallpaper. In a small space, you don't usually want contrasting colors. The doors are colored here only to illustrate the idea.

DOORS OPEN: Bedroom-Living Room

Illustrations by Roberta Sandenbergh and Alex Noble.

DOORS CLOSED: Undivided Living Room

FOLDOUT PARTITION WITH SHELF

Use a screen that becomes a bar or desk.

More Functions from Less Space
The more uses you can make out of a single article in your home, the more efficient your space will become.

Use a Foldout from a Foldout
In this case, a fold-down shelf attached to a folding screen can be used as a desk or a bar when the panels are folded out.

Buy a Folding Shelf Ready-made
There are many ready-made folding shelves on the market. Choose one that fits as flat as possible and is a maximum size of 2/3 of the panel's width.

Custom Example

In this design of a studio apartment in New York City by Michael K Chen Architects (MKCA), folding doors are used to close off a Murphy bed.

When the bed is up, the doors close, and a fold-down shelf is used as a bar in the living area. When the bed is down, the doors open out, and the shelf becomes a desk in the study area. The color of the Murphy bed doors matches the walls; everything blends in.

Photos courtesy of MKCA, Michael K Chen Architecture.

FOLDOUT PARTITION WITH A CHAIR

Use a screen that becomes a seat.

Turn a Screen into a High-Back Seat

A clever 2-for-1 foldout idea is a three-panel screen that turns itself into three tall-back dining chairs.

How It Works:

Each screen has a wooden frame with a full-length slot that allows lightweight panels to slide up and down and then fold and unfold into a chair position.

Custom Designed

This design by Daniel Milchtein is called the "Biombo Chair."

Design by Daniel Milchtein.

TRANSPARENT PARTITION

Hang up rods as a divider.

Have an Understated Solution
Just a few steel or wood rods can serve as a minimal divider.

Keep a Feeling of Spaciousness
Hanging rods from the ceiling divides the room but keeps a feeling of the entire room.

Photography by Mike Sinclair. Design by Hufft.

SHOJI PARTITION

Create elegant privacy.

A Guest Room in the Living Room

If all you need is an occasional guest room, consider making it part of your living room and dividing it off with sliding shoji panels. When the shoji panels slide all the way to an exterior wall, they provide good privacy for your guests.

Leave It Open Most of the Time

When the shoji screens slide back, the space magically opens up. Most of the time, you are adding an extra dimension to your living room, not making it look dinky or feel cramped by adding this extra function.

Design by Roberta Sandenbergh. Interiors by Sager & Associates. Photo by Hamish Niven.

SHOJIS CLOSED: Privacy for Bed Area

Photo by Wieland Gleich.

SHOJI PARTITION

SHOJIS OPEN: More Space for Living Area

MY STORY

Many years after I bought my small apartment in Cape Town, I received permission from the municipality to increase its size from 650 square feet (60m²) to 1050 square feet (98m²) by building an extension to the rear of the apartment. Using the space very carefully, my original 1-bed/1-bath flat became a 3-bed/ 2-bath apartment. This is one of the new bed spaces, divided off from the living room with floor-to-ceiling sliding shoji screens.

ROLLER BLIND PARTITION

Pull down window shade from the ceiling.

Clear the Floor

Partitions don't have to be on the floor. Roller blinds (or "window shades") can pull down from the ceiling to define a space.

Make It Heavy Duty

Window shades that are used as space dividers must be made of a thick heavy-duty fabric, with a metal bar sewn into the fabric at the bottom to give it the necessary weight.

Use It as a Projector Screen

A benefit of a roller shade space divider is to have a home theater available whenever you need a projector screen.

Clever Example

A space-compacting design by the Chinese architectural firm B.L.U.E. Studio is in an alley house in Beijing where the entire lot measures only 258 square feet (24 m^2)! It has a mattress that folds up to reveal a pop-up table and bench. The roller blinds pull up for dining and down for sleeping.

Bed with Side Cabinet

Bed with Privacy

Bed with Counter & Stools

Dining with Counter & Stools

ZIGZAG PARTITION

Make a private space for each child.

For a child, it isn't the amount of space that is important. It's the privacy that counts.

Cut Foam Mattress to Fit
If your bedroom is too small for standard mattresses, it's okay. Home Depot and other suppliers cut 4" (102mm) foam to fit. No child is 6'-3" (2m) tall.

Use Drywall Partitions
Use partitions that can be easily dismantled. You may not want this arrangement forever. And if you sell, the new owner may not like a divided bedroom. On the other hand, it might increase the house's value.

(a) Beds
In this scheme, one child has a normal bed with drawers underneath. The other has a loft bed built above a closet. To avoid a fight about who gets what, just say the older child gets the loft bed because he or she is less likely to fall off.

(b) Desk
The illustration indicates a long wall-mounted desk that continues behind the closets with a partition down the middle.

(c) Storage
The built-in closets are back-to-back, with shelves and a hanging rod. In this example, each closet is 48" (1219mm) wide, 48" (1219mm) high, and 20" (508mm) deep. In addition to the closets and the drawers under the bed, you can also install hooks along the walls for jackets, hats, and backpacks.

(d) Inside Window
Just for fun, put a window into the zigzag partition, as a "secret" way for the kids to communicate. When they aren't on speaking terms, they can just keep the window shut.

(e) Outside Windows
If the bedroom doesn't have two windows, you may have to put in a second one. If there's a large window, you can replace it with two smaller ones with the same opening size. Each half of the zigzag must have adequate ventilation.

(f) Doors
Although the partitions are flexible and can be dismantled, you do need an extra door to make the separation complete. The door can remain in place even if you remove the zigzag partition. Just keep it locked.

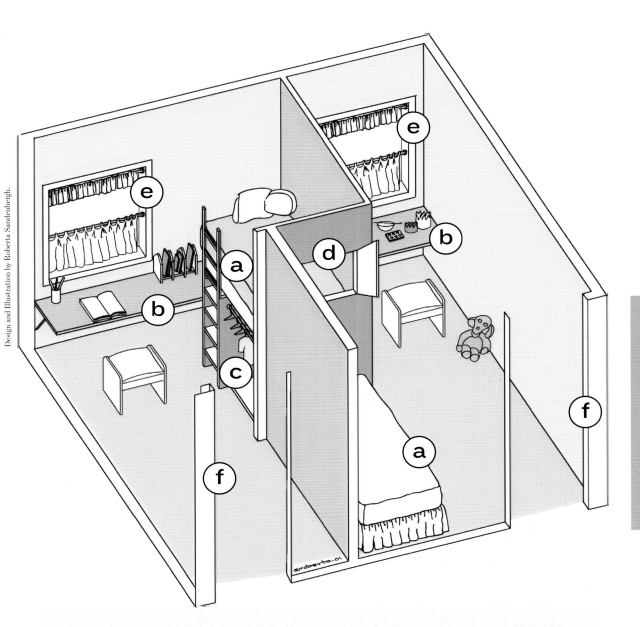

MY STORY

When we first arrived in South Africa, my daughter, Margot, went to a weekly boarding school. I took her to school on Monday mornings and picked her up on Friday afternoons. After two years, the school had to close its dormitory, and, rather than have her leave a school she loved, I agreed to have her stay during the week with her best friend, Fleur, who lived nearby. Fleur's mother divided a bedroom for the two girls, so each could have her own private space. It was her basic idea that led to this design.

U-SHAPED WALL PARTITION

Separate an alcove with a niche.

Use Depth for Privacy

Studio apartments or Junior-3s often feature an alcove to use as a bed, study, or dining space. Some people close it off completely; others keep it partially open. The depth of the U-shaped partition shown here gives the bed alcove extra privacy from the main room.

Use Extra Space on Both Sides

The U-shaped wall was used here to afford extra space for a dresser on the inside of the "U" in the bed area and a desk on the outside in the living room.

Mirror the Walls

For an unusual "fool-the-eye" effect, the sides of the alcove walls were mirrored on three sides to expand the space visually. (More in Chapter 10, Mirrored Spaces.)

MY STORY

My grown-up daughter lives in a studio apartment only a block away from me in Manhattan. Her apartment incorporates a U-shaped partition that conceals a queen-size bed from the living room but is open at the two ends for easy access. The U-shaped partition accommodates a chest of drawers on the inside of the "U" and a desk on the outside. Floor-to-ceiling mirrors are used on the three walls of the "U."

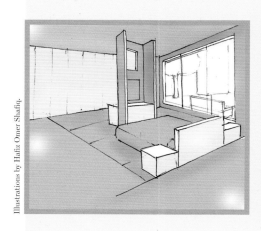

Illustrations by Hafiz Omer Shafiq.

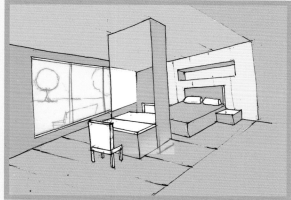

View from Bed Alcove

View from Living Room

SLIDING WALL PARTITION

Make a studio into 1-bedroom apartment.

A movable wall can transform a studio apartment into a one-bedroom when desired.

In this New York studio apartment designed by the firm Michael K Chen Architecture, different activities like entertaining, sleeping, and dressing are accommodated one at a time:

Closed Position
When the sliding partition is closed against the far bed wall, you have a spacious one-room studio or home office.

Halfway Position
When you slide the movable wall out halfway, there is a mirrored dressing room with a closet and built-in drawers.

Fully Extended Position
When the sliding wall is fully extended toward the living room side, a Murphy bed can pull down for a cozy little bedroom.

Two-Way Screen
This sliding partition wall is designed so that you can watch television and enjoy other media from both of its sides.

Dressing Area When Bed Is Up

4

CONVERTED SPACES

Create Airbnb Opportunities.

Convert a Home for Life Changes

Changes in your life can lead to making changes in your home.
For example, you may choose to convert your home when:

- *A grown child leaves*
- *A grown child returns*
- *A parent needs a home*
- *You need a home aide*

Convert a Home for Income

Many people are doing home conversions in order to accommodate long-term tenants or short-term guests. Having short-term guests (nowadays via Airbnb) involves changing linen and perhaps providing coffee, tea, and snacks—but it can be very profitable.

Convert a Home for Real Estate Value

You may not need the extra living space for yourself. But if you are planning to sell your home, a real estate agent may well advise you to convert part of your home into a separate apartment. The increased real estate value will usually be far more than the construction cost, especially if you are willing to do some of the work yourself.

Best Candidates for Space Conversion:

- *Closets*
- *Hallways*
- *Master Bedrooms*
- *Garages*
- *Attics*
- *Basements*
- *Maids' Rooms*

Best Candidates for Space Division:

- *A Home with at least Two Bathrooms*
- *A Home with Two Entrances*
- *A Home with an Entry Hall*

ATTIC INTO APARTMENT

Make better use of this storage area.

Attics are good candidates for conversion to apartments but require special attention to building codes and ventilation.

Potential Problems:

- Access and Egress
- Ceiling Height
- Creaking Floors
- Ventilation and Insulation

Find Out about Access and Egress

Some codes stipulate that, for fire safety, there should be two ways out: a second staircase or a window, for example. They also require a full-size staircase 3' (900mm) wide.

Consider Ceiling Height

Codes usually require staircases with a 6'–8" clearance height. Some also require living spaces with a 7'–0" headroom over 70 square feet. This may mean that only part of your attic can be legally converted, although the low areas can be used for storage.

Fix Creaking Floors

Attic floors generally need reinforcement with additional joists to keep from creaking. It's also best to use a plywood subfloor before finishing the floor with wood or tile.

Install Ventilation and Insulation

Attics often have excess heat and moisture. Windows at each end will promote cross ventilation, but you may still need air conditioning and/or fans. A layer of spray foam insulation under the roof and in the walls can help cut heating and cooling costs.

Use Sloped Roof as a Motif

A sloped roof of an attic may limit headroom, but it can also be an interesting design motif.

Photography by Terence Tourangeau. Design by Tact Design.

ATTIC INTO APARTMENT

SINGLE BEDROOM INTO APARTMENT

Convert closets into bathroom and minikitchen.

Even a single bedroom can be converted into a separate apartment.

What to Look For:

- A closet that can be converted into a bathroom or minikitchen.
- A hallway that can serve as an entry foyer to both apartments.
- Empty wall space for new closets to replace the old ones.

Closet into Bathroom

The living-room closet became the bathroom for the larger apartment.

Closet into Kitchen

The bedroom closet became the kitchen for the smaller apartment.

Partition for Bed Area

A partition wall separated a new bed space from the old living area.

Hallway into Entry

The old hallway in between the living room and bedroom became the common entry for the two new units.

New Closets

One new closet for each unit replaced the converted closets.

MY STORY

A neighbor in my apartment building, a single woman who wanted extra income, asked me to draw up plans so her apartment could accommodate a tenant. There was only one bedroom, one bathroom, and one entry door—but it had a very large hallway in between the living room and the bedroom. This was the key to the conversion: the hallway became the joint access for the two new units. A living room closet became a bathroom, and a bedroom closet became a minikitchen; a new door was installed between the hall and the living room; and a partition was added to make a bed area.

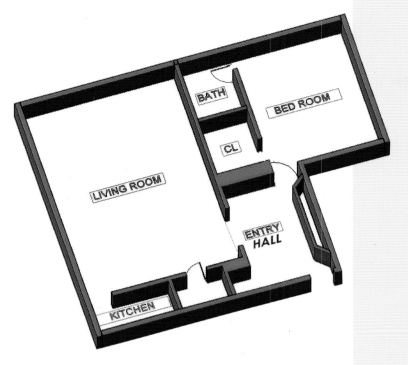

BEFORE: One-Bedroom Apartment

Illustrations by Hafiz Omer Shafiq.

AFTER: Studio Apartment and Guest Apartment

HALLWAY INTO APARTMENT

Deep closet for sleeping, storage, and dining.

Fit Everything into a Long Closet

Use half of the room's width for a long, deep closet. The other half will be a corridor to access the closet.

Slide Everything In and Out

Design it like a Swiss Army knife where everything slides in and out.
For example:

- A Slide-Out Bookcase as a Stair to a Sleeping Loft.
- A Slide-Out Dining Table and Chairs that fold up under the table.
- Slide-Out Closets and Drawer Cabinets.

Put Bathroom in the Corner

A tiny bathroom can be an extension of the slide-out closet and the same depth.

Put Kitchen between Bathroom and Entry Door

A kitchen with a foldout counter over the sink and stove can go under a window in between the bathroom and the entry door.

Example

Maids' rooms have largely disappeared in America but still exist on the top floors of European apartment houses. The conversion shown here is of a tiny 8-square-meter (86-square-foot) maid's room in Paris. It was designed by Kitoko Studio.

All photos on 94 and 95 by Fabienne Delafraye. Designed by Kitoko Studio.

**Closet
Hallway**

**Sleeping
Loft**

**Slide-Out
Wardrobe**

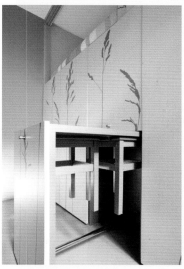

**Table and
Chairs**

**Bookcase
as Stairway**

**Bathroom
Corner**

GARAGE INTO APARTMENT

Increase the value of your home.

Tenant vs. Car

It may be a question of which you need the most: extra income or a home for your car. You may reasonably decide that your car could survive living on the street, whereas you probably could not.

Perfect Size

A typical 2-car garage is 484 ft^2 (45m^2) or 22 feet x 22 feet (6.7m x 6.7m), a perfect size for a small apartment.

Or Consider an Above-Garage Apartment

A more ambitious project is to remove the roof of the garage completely and build a second story for rental purposes.

Use the Garage Door

If you decide to leave the door openings as is, you can fit them with attractive double doors (as shown). Otherwise, you must fix them in a shut position, insulate them and seal the edges. An alternative is to install a large bay window in one of the door openings.

Fill In Exterior Wall

If you remove the door, fill in the opening with a frame wall covered with sheet rock. To reduce heating and cooling costs, install insulation or fiberglass underneath.

Finish Interior Walls

Paint the walls prior to installing any flooring. Work from the top down: ceiling first, then the walls. A high-pressure paint sprayer will cut painting time down by at least 2/3.

Get the Permits

Before you begin, check with your local zoning ordinance as to what permits they require. As a minimum, you will need permits for the electric wiring and plumbing. A building inspector must review the property before it can be rented or inhabited.

Decide On Heating and Cooling

You will usually have to buy a separate space heater and air conditioner. But you could also connect the new unit to the temperature control features of your house. Compare the daily wattage used by these devices to your existing heating and cooling bill to help you decide which is more economical.

Install Wiring and Pipes

You need at least four electrical outlets and separate plumbing from the house. Try to keep the bathroom and kitchen close to the shared wall between the new unit and the house. The farther the wiring and pipes have to travel, the more expensive it will be.

Finish the Floor

Add a thin layer of concrete to level the floor and use a garage floor cleaner. Install baseboards, caulked to the wall and the floor. After painting the walls and ceiling, it is advisable to clean the floor again. Use ceramic or vinyl tiles. Wall-to-wall carpeting is not recommended for garages.

Design by Beth Dana.

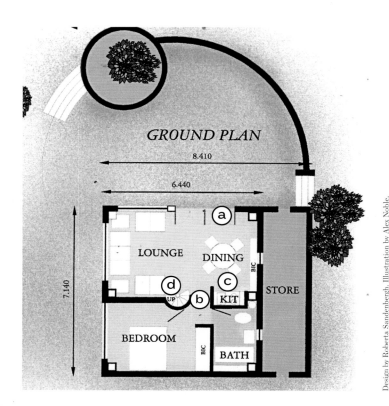

GROUND PLAN

8.410

6.440

7.140

LOUNGE

DINING

(a)

(d)

UP

(b)

(c)

KIT

BIC

STORE

BEDROOM

BIC

BATH

Design by Roberta Sandenbergh. Illustration by Alex Noble.

Tips for Converting Garage

(a) No Entry Area

To save space, I designed the cottage without a formal entry area. You enter directly into an open living area from a courtyard.

(b) No Hallway

You go straight through the living area to a small alcove with two doors in the back. One door leads to a bedroom, the other to a bathroom. We didn't need a hallway.

(c) No Real Kitchen

A closet-size alcove hides a mini-kitchen behind double doors with shallow storage baskets. (See Chapter 1, Closet Spaces, page 13.)

(d) Add a Loft Bedroom

The high roof allows for a sleeping loft above the bedroom and bathroom, for which I built a spiral staircase around a steel pole. (See Chapter 5, Stacked Spaces, page 107.)

MY STORY

When I bought my five-acre property in South Africa, I didn't even know it had a garage. It was near the back fence and covered with vines. After the vines were cleared away, I saw that it was a wonderful structure with thick stone pillars and a pitched thatch roof, the size of a large studio apartment. I could see it would make a wonderful cottage; the problem was finding the money to build it. The solution drove up one day in a bright red car. A beautiful young woman with long dark hair stepped out and said in a thick accent: "I loave thees place. I want to leeve here." Her name was Sara, and she was a Portuguese refugee from Mozambique. She and her boyfriend, Vasco, moved in with me, and I used their rent money to build my cottage. I found a wonderful African builder named Zaccharia who said he could build anything. He was very old and slow, but this suited me just fine. Ordering materials only when I had the money, I took almost a year to finish the cottage. When it was finally finished, I moved in with my eight-year-old daughter: I slept in the loft and my daughter in the small bedroom underneath. It was just like a Soho loft apartment, but under a thatch roof:

Photo by D. Allen SA.

MASTER BEDROOM INTO APARTMENT

Convert dressing room into kitchen.

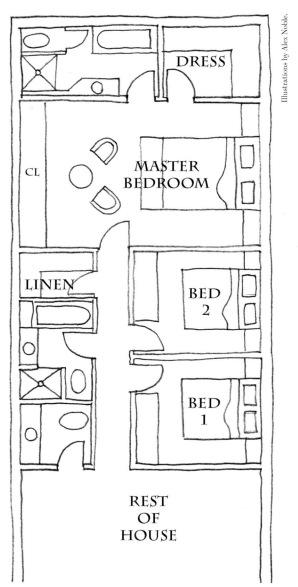

Illustrations by Alex Noble.

DRESS

CL

MASTER BEDROOM

LINEN

BED 2

BED 1

REST
OF
HOUSE

BEFORE: Master Bedroom and Two Bedrooms

MY STORY

A good friend in South Africa lived with her husband in a very large house. When they divorced, she received the house as part of the divorce settlement. With a reduced income, she struggled to maintain it. I suggested she convert the master bedroom suite into a rental apartment. I drew up plans, leaving the bathroom "as is" and converting the dressing room into a kitchen. There was an exterior door, so the new tenants didn't have to go through the rest of the house.

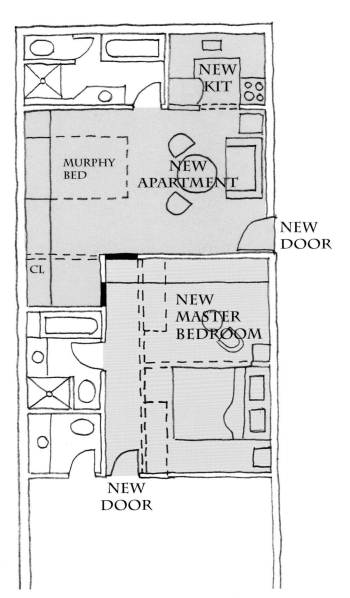

NEW KIT

MURPHY BED

NEW APARTMENT

NEW DOOR

CL

NEW MASTER BEDROOM

NEW DOOR

AFTER: New Apartment and New Master Bedroom

Combine Small Bedrooms
Small bedrooms and a bathroom can be combined to become a new master bedroom attached to the rest of the house. This leaves the original master bedroom free to become a separate apartment.

Use What's Already There
A master bedroom suite already has closets and a bathroom. They can usually be reused as is.

Convert Dressing Area into Kitchen
If the suite has a dressing room or alcove, it could become a mini-kitchen.

Create Private Access
If it's possible to add an exterior door, it not only increases the value of your accommodation, it will make having "guests" in your home less intrusive.

SPLIT A HOUSE IN TWO
Divide for family or income.

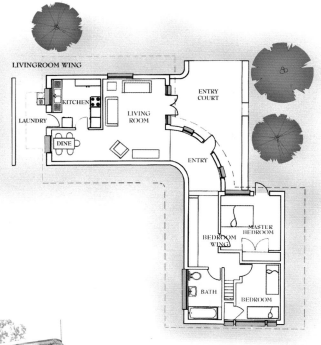

LIVINGROOM WING

KITCHEN

LAUNDRY

DINE

LIVING ROOM

ENTRY COURT

ENTRY

MASTER BEDROOM

BEDROOM WING

BATH

BEDROOM

Illustrations on this and the following page by Alex Noble.

BEFORE: One House

Cottage One

MY STORY

After I converted a garage into a cottage, I decided to divide the main house into two separate units. The plan of the house was in the shape of an "L," so it lent itself well to being divided. The living/kitchen area *became one unit, the bedroom/bath area the other. My plan was to rent out my garage-cottage and move into the living room/ kitchen section of the house. A dusty attic over the kitchen became my sleeping loft. It meant taking down a high wall and made a mountain of dust. But it morphed into such a glamorous space that I wanted to sleep up there even before the floor was finished. Unfortunately, I got up from the bed on the*

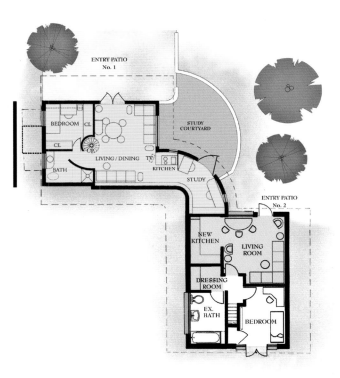

AFTER: Two Cottages

Unit 1:

- **Attic** over the Kitchen became a **Bedroom**.
- **Kitchen** with Exterior Door became a **Bedroom**.
- **Dining Nook** became a **Bathroom**.
- **Entry Hall** became a **Home Office**.

Unit 2:

- **Master Bedroom** became a **Living Room**.
- **Corridor** became a **Kitchen**.
- **Bathroom, Bedroom & Loft Stair** remained as is.

Cottage Two

side where the floor wasn't finished and fell straight down into the new bathroom! Luckily, the second section was much easier to convert. I just demolished the wall between the master bedroom and the corridor; with the corridor gone, the bedroom became a living room. The back bedroom, the bathroom, and a second loft remained just as they were. So it was ready to rent out in little more than a month. As soon as the first unit had a toilet, I moved in and used the rental income to finish it up.

IDEA 37.

SPLIT AN APARTMENT IN TWO

Convert closets and the hallway.

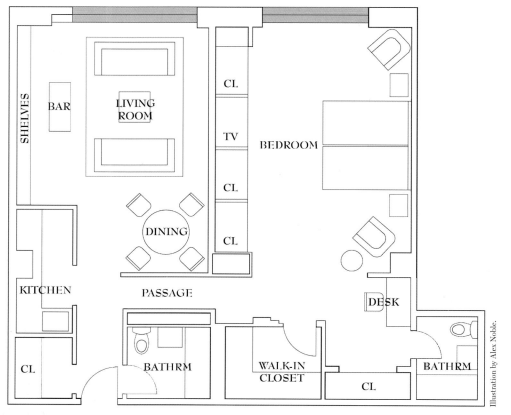

Illustration by Alex Noble.

BEFORE: One One-Bedroom Apt

MY STORY

When I moved back to New York after living in South Africa for 20 years (and dividing several houses there), I searched for a Manhattan apartment I could divide. Luckily, I found a large 1-bedroom apartment with 2 bathrooms and 2 entrance doors. I bought it with all the furniture, with the intention of dividing it into 2 studios. I found a brilliant carpenter named Zack Sullivan through the Yellow Pages and was able to turn a walk-in closet into a kitchen, a 2-door closet into a Murphy bed, and a hallway into new closets. This is how it worked:

Divided Apartment

APARTMENT 1

APARTMENT 2

CL

CL

EX. KITCHEN

CL   CL

(a)

CL

EX. BATHROOM

NEW BAR KITCHEN

(b)

EX. BATH

(c)

(d)

Illustration by Alex Noble.

AFTER: Two Equal Studio Apts

Convert the Closets
Look for closets that can be converted into minikitchens or bathrooms.

(a) Hallway into Closet
The hallway between the living room and bedroom became two closets to form a soundproof divider between the apartments.

(b) Walk-in Closet into Kitchen
A bar in the original living room had a fridge, counter, drawers, glass shelves, and a mirrored back wall. So all it needed was a sink, cooktop, and electric outlets after it was moved into a walk-in closet to become the new kitchen of one of the studios.

Use the Hallways
Look for hallways that can be used for access, storage, or division.

(c) Single Beds into Divans
The king-size bed in the bedroom was separated into two single beds to become a long sofa in the other studio.

(d) Closet as Murphy Bed
One of the double-door closets in the bedroom became a Murphy bed (see Chapter 1: Closet Spaces). The doors were hinged at one side, so when the bed came down, the doors fanned out to create a partition from the rest of the apartment.

5

STACKED SPACES

Don't forget the vertical dimension.

Think of Air Rights

When New York City real estate developers talk about air rights, they refer to empty space above a building. In a bizarre twist of property law, these empty spaces can be bought and sold to gain extra floor space for other buildings.

Look For Vertical Spaces

You can use the same principal in your house or apartment. The footprint on the ground may be limited, but you may have valuable vertical space right above it. You just have to look for it.

Stack Things Up

Think of bunk beds: stacking kids in double or even triple bunks. In the same way, you could stack a bed or a play loft over a desk, a table over another table, a bookshelf over a window, or a bed over a kitchen.

PLAY LOFT OVER DESK

Keep kids safe and toys off the floor.

Keep a Toddler Safe

If you work at home after your baby is born, you could put a playpen near your desk. But babies soon become toddlers, and you could roll backward and accidentally run over a little crawler. What you need is a space where you can keep an eye on your child, but not too close to your chair: maybe a ***play loft***.

Become Work Buddies

Kids love to feel grown up. So when you are doing your work downstairs, they can do theirs upstairs. You glance up from your computer and smile; they look down from their coloring book and wave. With a play loft, you and your child can become work buddies.

Don't Bump Your Head

You won't be able to stand up underneath a play loft, so you have to roll backward before getting up. It takes a bit of practice, but, eventually, you will learn to roll back and stand up in one motion and never bump your head.

Put a Mattress at the Bottom

Eventually, toddlers learn to go up and down a ladder by themselves. So keep a thick mattress at the bottom.

Ready-made

Many so-called "loft beds" come equipped with a desk underneath the bed. If you start with one of these, you will have to add a few things like a safety gate and wall/floor supports. None may be perfect when it arrives from the store, but it beats making one from scratch—and some ready-made units even come with stairs to go up and a slide to come down.

Or DIY

If you're a handy person or have a handy husband, you can make a play loft yourself with 4 x 4 posts, 2 x 6 floor joists, and ¾" plywood. Add 2 x 2 bracing at the corners, steel angles at the floor for extra support, and a fascia for a finished look. Here are a few tips:

(a) Floor Finish

Finish the play loft floor with soft carpeting or a thin piece of foam.

(b) Lights and Plugs

Lights attached to the bottom of the loft are a good way to light up your desk. You can also add ceiling lights, but definitely no wall lights within reach of the play loft occupant. Same thing goes for electric plugs.

(c) Ladder

You may start out carrying your toddler up and down the ladder. So make it sturdy, at least 1" (25mm) thick, with treads no more than 10" (254mm) apart. Make sure it's secure bottom and top.

Illustration by Roberta Sandenbergh and Alex Noble.

Railing
d

Make sure it has a smooth finish.
Even add a crib rail cover. Secure
the rail to at least one wall with
small steel angles.

Safety Gate
e

Attach a safety gate at the top of
the ladder and keep it locked.

BED OVER DESK

Buy one or make it yourself.

Ready-made

These stand-alone pieces of furniture are sold ready-to-assemble by retail outlets. The compact structure shown here is by Pottery Barn's *PBteen* and has a narrow desk and bookshelves underneath a bed accessible by a ladder.

Best for Teenagers

They are marketed mostly to teenagers, who are attracted by the private place that it offers to hide away from everybody.

DIY

A hobbyist could adapt the general idea and make one of these desk-beds out of pieces of plywood.

Product Photo courtesy of PBTeen.

BED OVER STORAGE
Use for kids, teens, and adults.

Okay for Kids
This is a fun way to teach kids to take care of their things. Just make the ladder easy to climb.

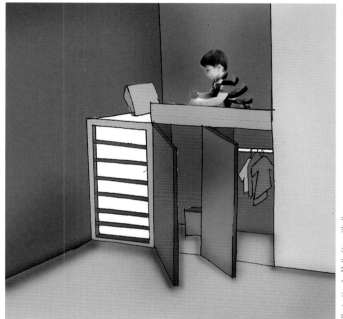

Illustration by Hafiz Omer Shafiq.

But Ideal for Teenagers
A closet bed offers space for a large teenage wardrobe (hanging and folded) with extra storage in the "step-drawers."

Product Photo courtesy of Foter.

BED-DESK OVER STORAGE

Make an all-in-one bedroom.

Create Privacy in a Compact Space

Everyone in your household, especially a teenager, deserves a private space—but it need not be an entire room. It could be small enough to fit into an alcove or even a hallway. The sketch shows a space less than 6' x 6' (1.8m x 1.8m).

- **Start with the Mattress**
  If you don't have enough room for a twin-size mattress, order a 4" (102mm)-thick foam mattress to your child's or teenager's height. They are available online.

- **Look for Standard Units**
  There are small cabinets, desks, and shelves at Ikea and many other retail outlets.

- **Close Up Back of Desk**
  Add a board to the back of the desk for safety (not shown in illustration).

- **Find a Handyman**
  You will need a handyman-cum-carpenter to put it all together: a closet base for the bed, a door at one end, a board for the back of desk, and a small stair or ladder.

Illustration by Hafiz Omer Shafiq.

BED OVER KITCHEN & BATHROOM

Sleep over back of apartment.

Compact All the Services
Before you start this kind of renovation, it is best to make sure all the service components (bathroom, kitchen, and closets) are compacted into as small a space as possible at one side of the apartment.

Check Ceiling Height Regulations
You have to check whether or not your local municipality counts a kitchen or bathroom as a living space with a minimum ceiling height. If not, you should lower the ceiling to gain as much height for your loft as possible.

Get Used to Low Sleeping Area
If you can't reduce the ceiling height below the sleeping loft, you may have to resign yourself to a low space not high enough to even sit up in. But hey, who sits up when they're sleeping? (If you're really worried about hitting your head, wear a helmet.)

Install Closet on the Stairs
If there is enough room, a good place to build extra closets (some of which may be reduced when you do your renovation) is on a stair landing halfway up to the loft.

Install Strip Kitchen
If you can change around the layout and location of your kitchen, the best solution will often be a strip kitchen just below the loft with narrow folding doors that can hide it away from the rest of the living area.

Use White Walls
Painting everything white will expand and unify the space.

Example
These photos are from a 300-sq.-ft. apartment designed by architects Beriot, Bernardini.

Design by Beriot, Bernardini architects. Photography by Yen Chen.

BED OVER A KITCHEN

Sleep over the cabinets.

Use the Upper Cabinet Space

Many studio apartments have surprisingly big kitchens, more than you may need if you are a single person who lives on takeout, for example. So using some of the upper cabinet space could be the answer to the difficult question: "Where do I put the bed?"

- **Line Up the Bed with the Cabinets**
  The underside of the shallow cabinets above a kitchen counter is usually at a good height for the top of a bed. So line them up so they look like they belong together.

- **Fit Storage Underneath**
  You can use the underside of the bed for storage (perhaps hanging clothes on rods or folded on shelves), but access it from other sides of the room—not from the kitchen side.

- **Create a Partition**
  You will need a partition at least from the kitchen side of the bed to avoid food odors and perhaps smoke. You can use a clear pane of glass as in this example, but a curtain would add some privacy.

- **Use a Platform**
  To make it easy to get in and out of bed, use a short ladder onto a platform, rather than trying to get into bed directly from a ladder. Bed making will also be easier.

MY STORY

When I was practicing as an architect in South Africa, a client asked me to redesign the standard plan of a "development house" before he moved in, so he could accommodate his grown son when he came to visit. The house was small and so were the bedrooms. The only place I could find for a sleeping area was over the kitchen. So I designed a loft ceiling over the kitchen with a staircase from the living room (the "lounge," as it was called). The builder accepted the redesign and just added the cost of the loft as an "extra" to the house price. Sometime later I was astonished to discover that the developer had added a "kitchen loft model" to the list of available house models!

In this open one-room apartment in central
Stockholm, architect Karin Matz used standard
IKEA units to build in a bed alcove the kitchen
cabinets. Just a clear pane of glass separates the
bed from the kitchen area, but a curtain could
add more privacy. This design idea gives new
meaning to having breakfast in bed!

STACK UNDER TABLES
Pull stuff out only when company comes.

Store "Once-In-A-While" Stuff

"Getting social" means you may suddenly need extra stuff to accommodate guests: tables, seats, maybe some china. These items are so rarely used that you may feel they don't deserve a 365-day home in a cabinet or closet.

ⓐ Plexiglas Table(s) under Glass Table

You can order custom-made Plexiglas tables from a company called Plexicraft. Leave at least a 2" (51mm) height between tables so you can pull them out easily.

ⓑ Stash Papers Dust-Free

The narrow spaces between the tables can be used to stash newspapers and magazines. If the tables are glass or Plexiglas, you can see what's in there.

ⓒ Use Seats as Footrests

When not being used by guests, cushion seats can serve as footrests for lounging on the sofa.

ⓓ Decorative China under Table

Keep good china safe and handy underneath a glass table.

ⓔ Use Stacked Side Tables

Low stacked tables can serve as extra tables or seats for a cozy area around your sofa.

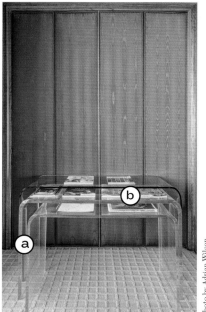

Photo by Adrian Wilson.

Stacked Plexiglas Tables under Glass Desk

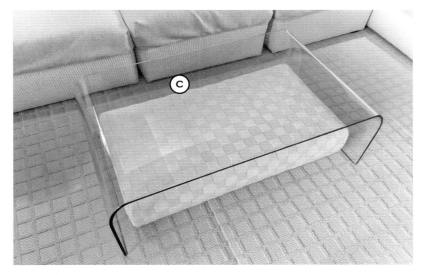

Stacked Floor Cushion Seats under Glass Coffee Table

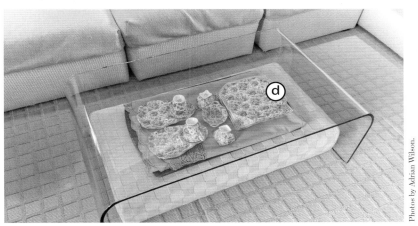

SHELVES ABOVE A ROOM

Learn to use a grabber pole.

As a Unifying Element

Shelves near the ceiling add a unifying and decorative design element to your living spaces.

As Low-Cost Storage

An overhead shelf has the lowest rent value in your entire home. It's the perfect place for things you rarely use but can't face throwing away. As in Chapter 1: Closet Spaces, use large labels on boxes so you can read them from below.

For Books and Ornaments

There's hardly a door, window, or wall that doesn't offer shelf space overhead for books and ornaments.

Illustration by Roberta Sandenbergh and Alex Noble.

SPIRAL STAIR POLE

Better than a ladder—more than a pole.

It's a good idea to stack up your spaces, but going easily from one level to the next may require more than a ladder. Here's an alternative:

Use a Pole Stair
You can fit a stair into an incredibly tight space with a steel pole secured to the floor and steps spiraling around it.

Buy One Factory-Made
A few ready-made spiral stair poles are on the market. This model is from the Italian company Interbau Solutions.

Or DIY
All you need is a steel pipe and brackets, thick pieces of wood with holes in them, and a tube of epoxy.

Courtesy of Interbau.

Do-It-Yourself Pole Stair

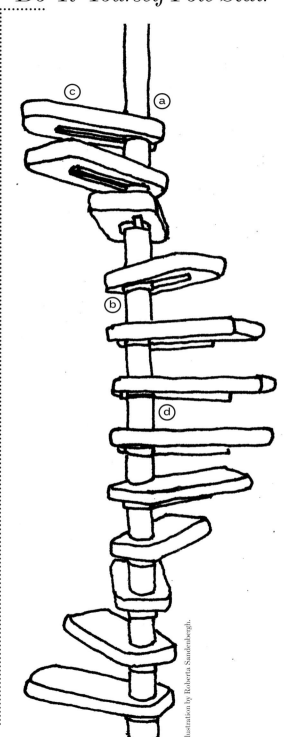

Illustration by Roberta Sandenbergh.

Secure Pipe

ⓐ Get a steel pipe that is about 3' (914mm) longer than the floor-to-floor height and attach it securely to the floor (or into the ground).

Mark Supports

ⓑ Divide the pipe by the number of steps required floor-to floor and mark the positions on the pole. Make a cross wherever the middle of a step intersects the mark.

Cut out Steps

ⓒ Draw a full-size plan of one step with a cutout hole for the pipe at one end. Use 2" (51mm)-pine with rounded edges.

Attach Brackets and Steps

ⓓ Position the first steel bracket at the bottom at the cross mark. Drop a step down from the top and screw it in from the bottom. Drop the next and the next, until you reach the top.

Check Building Regulations

Spiral pole stairs like this one will probably not meet building department requirements, especially if they don't have a handrail and 3' (914mm)-wide treads. I suggest that you use this idea only for yourself and perhaps some adventurous guests.

MY STORY

I first got the idea for a pole stair when I built a sleeping loft in a converted garage in South Africa. There was no space for a normal spiral stair and I didn't want to use a ladder, so I thought about the kind of poles used by firemen. I chose to use a pole—one with steps, but without a handrail. I learned to climb those stairs at a terrific clip—up to my bed and down to the bathroom—sometimes several times a night. I would just hold onto the pole! I slept up there for over twenty years and never once fell down. My little cockapoo Freeway wasn't so successful. After she fell down a couple of times, she chose to sleep in a soft doggie bed at the bottom of the stairs.

Photos by Roberta Sandenbergh.

VERTICAL HOUSE

Climb round and round a fireplace.

A Solution for Small Lots
If you have limited space on the ground, you have little choice but to think vertical.

Put the Staircase in the Middle
A staircase in the middle of a house is a simple way to gain equal access to your floor levels. You could think of the different levels as spokes leading out from the staircase.

Design and illustrations by Roberta Sandenbergh.

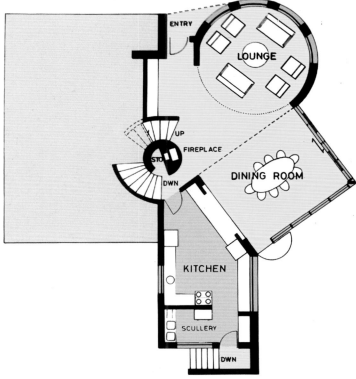

Y STORY

client in South Africa asked me to design a house on a small
bdivided parcel of land that had a swimming pool. He was a
chelor interested in fitness who wanted to keep the pool for his
rly-morning swim. So with the pool taking up so much space on
e small property, it didn't leave much room for a house. I had to
nk "vertical" and designed a house that kept going up a spiral
aircase around a stone fireplace. There were four levels, where
ch one was open to the one below. The house was so unusual
it it was featured in House & Garden magazine.

Photos by Roberta Sandenbergh.

6

WALL SPACES

A wall is more than a space divider.

This Is Valuable Real Estate

I suggest that, at least for the time you are reading this chapter, you start to think of your walls not as places to hang pictures, but as valuable real estate.

Take Down Your Pictures

If you're tight for space, you should use walls for more practical purposes than hanging up prints and posters. And you can always put these on the ceiling. See Chapter 9: Ceiling Spaces (page 173).

Hang Stuff on the Wall

Hang up your chairs. Get your kids to hang up their toys. Hang up shallow closets.

Build Stuff into the Wall

Use your walls to carve out niches for your books, clothes, and art objects.

IDEA 48.

CHAIRS ON THE WALL

Do what the Shakers do.

Declutter Your Life

Removing clutter from the floor was the Shakers' way of living a simple life. Not a bad idea for any society.

Clear the Floor

Create space and simplify floor cleaning by hanging up your chairs. You will suddenly find room to move around!

Use All of Your Walls

You needn't put up pegs in just the table areas. Place pegs along all the walls and hang up chairs wherever they happen to be. A folding chair needs nothing more than a sturdy hook.

Create a Design

Make a pattern of the chairs on the wall for an interesting kind of decoration. (The chairs in the photo on the right are the Hiroshima chairs from Maruni Wood Industry.)

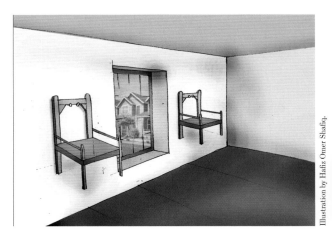

Illustration by Hafiz Omer Shafiq.

Courtesy of Maruni.

Photo courtesy of BigStock.

TABLE ON THE WALL

Pull down a picture.

Eliminate a 24-Hour Floor Space
A table used only for meals or large gatherings needn't take up a 24-hour floor space.

Ready-made
There are fold-down tables on the market with pictures or mirrors applied to their backs and legs tucked in.

Movable
The model shown here is by ivydesign-furniture.com and allows you to fold down the table and move it away from the wall to accommodate more chairs.

BEFORE: Picture on Wall

Design and Photography by Verena Lang.

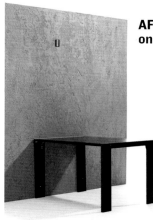

AFTER: Table on Floor

DESK ON THE WALL

Fold down a laptop.

Find a Place on a Wall that Spells "Work"

Nowadays you don't need a study—you don't even need a desk. You can plop down a laptop anywhere—on a kitchen table or even a bed—but it helps psychologically to have a specific work place, no matter how minute. See Chapter 1: Office in a Closet.

Have a Hideaway for Papers

A fold-down desk attached to a wall hides away your papers when it's up and allows you to work when it's down.

Buy Ready-mades

This needn't be a DIY project. There are plenty of ready-made models available. The one shown here is from Ligne Roset.

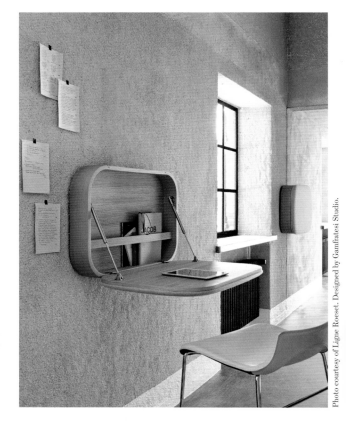

Photo courtesy of Ligne Roset. Designed by Gamfratesi Studio.

TOYS ON THE WALL
Use baskets, bins, or buckets.

DIY or Ready-made
Make them out of baskets, bins, or buckets and paint them different colors. Or buy them ready-made like this one designed by Jessie Rivers.

Keep Them Low to the Floor
The easier to get at, the more they will be used. Encourage your kids to put their toys away by themselves.

Involve Your Kids
Let the kids help you when you put them up. Let them decide which kinds of toys go in which container.

Photo courtesy of Jessie Rivers.

SHALLOW CLOSET ON WALL
Think of a clothing store.

Hang Clothes Parallel to Wall

You don't need a deep space to hang clothes parallel to the wall. A few inches will accommodate your everyday outfits hung up this way—just like in a clothing store.

Close Off with Window Shades or Curtains

Instead of doors, hide your clothes with curtains or decorative shades, which don't take up any space at all.

Double Stack

You can hang two layers of garments on the wall, one above the other. However, you may need a grabber pole for long dresses.

Ready-made

There are a few ready-made shallow closets on the market. But as apartments get smaller and smaller, I'm sure we will be seeing more of them.

DIY

You can make a simple 12" (305mm) plywood frame for a hallway "closet." Put up a short rod perpendicular to the wall.

Add Shelves

Handbags and folded items also fit into a shallow space. Shelves can be above the hanging rod. Add cubbyholes at the bottom for shoes and boots.

Turn a Hallway into a Dressing Room

You can fit a closet that is only 10" (254mm) or 12" (305mm) deep into most hallways. In this way, you can turn an otherwise wasted space into a dressing room.

Illustration by Alex Noble.

Illustration by Hafiz Omer Shafiq.

MY STORY

After my husband and I sacrificed our one and only bedroom closet to make a baby room, we had to find other places to put our clothes. So we put up coat rods, hung our clothes parallel to the wall, and hid them away with curtains from the ceiling. In the entry hall, we built shallow frames for coats and boots behind decorative window shades. We used every last inch of wall space in that apartment. Yes, it was a lot of work. But no, we didn't have to move right away.

Photo by John Sandenbergh.

CABINET ON THE WALL

Hang doors from the ceiling.

Use Shallow Shelves

You can pack in masses of stuff on very shallow 8" (203mm) shelves going all the way up to the ceiling.

Hide It Away

Folding doors on a sliding track in the ceiling can hide everything away.

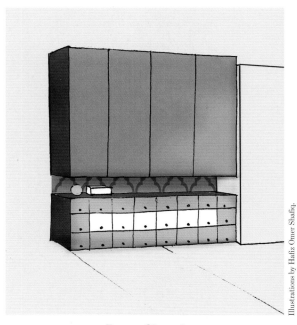

Doors Closed

Illustrations by Hafiz Omer Shafiq.

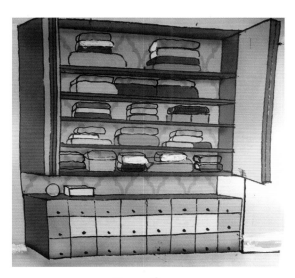

Doors Open

MY STORY

For our Greenwich Village bedroom, my husband and I bought an old apothecary chest at auction, just 12" (305mm) deep. It became a filing cabinet par excellence for everything from socks and underwear to scarves and gloves. Above the chest, we built a stack of shelves, closed off with folding doors from the ceiling. It looked wonderfully tidy when the doors were closed. When the doors were open, it was more like a colorful Oriental Bazaar.

Doors Closed with Lights

Photos by John Sandenbergh.

Doors Open with Lights and Flowers

STROLLER OR BICYCLE ON THE WALL

Hang it up in between rides.

Get It off the Floor

Strollers and bicycles are awkward contraptions that don't really deserve a space in a small home—not even in a closet. So hang it up.

Make It Convenient

The scenario is: "Open door. Reach up. Hang up." It has to be made quick and easy. Otherwise, the stroller or bike will remain on the floor, in everyone's way.

Use the Back of a Door

If you can't find a spare wall in your entry hall, use the back of a door.

Photo courtesy of Kiddies Kingdom UK.

Design by Szymon Hanczar. Photography by Jedrzej Stelmaszek.

GARDEN ON THE WALL

Create a green space.

An indoor garden wall is not only beautiful, but also improves the air quality in the room. Besides turning carbon dioxide into oxygen, plants also absorb harmful gases produced by sprays, fabrics, rugs, plastics, and cigarettes.

Use Dark Wall
Put up dark planters to match the color of the wall.

Layer the Plants
Use different rows for different kinds of plants.

Low Maintenance
Place plants such as succulents, low ground cover, and ferns high up on the wall.

Absorbent Floor Mat
Add a floor mat at the bottom of the wall to absorb water.

Courtesy of ZOOCO ESTUDIO Madrid. Photo by Orlando Gutiérrez.

IDEA 56.

NICHE IN A WALL

Hollow out spaces for books & ornaments.

Use Spaces in between Wood Studs

The standard spacing of a wood stud wall in the U.S. is 16" and sometimes as much as 24". This gives you an opportunity to carve out spaces in between the studs for books, clothes, or decorative objects.

Chop Out Brick Walls

With brick walls, chopping out a niche means using a sledge hammer and an angle grinder—and making a cloud of red dust. But, at least for me, it was worth doing.

If Possible—Do It during Construction

Figure out where you want your wall niches while you are building or renovating. This will be far cheaper and easier than chopping them out later.

Designed by Tali Hardonag, architect.

Photos by D. Allen SA.

MY STORY

My house in South Africa had a thatch roof that came down so low you couldn't even walk next to most of the walls. So I didn't have enough wall space for bookcases. My solution was to hollow out sections of the low brick wall that ran along the back of the house. When the builder started using an angle grinder to cut into the bricks, I couldn't even look. Sparks flew everywhere, and I thought the roof would catch on fire. It created a terrible mess and there was red dust everywhere. In the end, however, it created a lovely line of book titles that snaked along the entire length of the house.

KID ON THE WALL

Curl up in a bookcase.

Hide in Plain Sight

Kids love to have a secret place to hide away with a favorite book. But sometimes there's no room for a hideaway—not even a closet or a corner. This wheel should feel like a hideaway even though it's clearly in plain sight.

DIY

Just clear away some books, fit a kid-size wheel or tire in between bookshelves, and line it with a comfortable soft cushion. Not much work to make a child very happy.

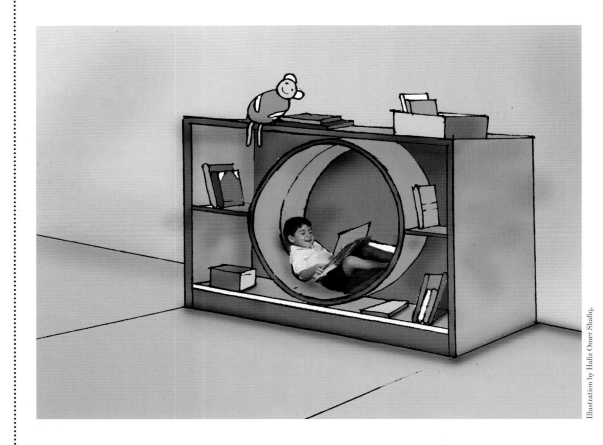

Illustration by Hafiz Omer Shafiq.

BEDS IN THE WALL

Take inspiration from a boat cabin.

Fool the Eye
Building a bed into the wall makes a bedroom feel larger than it is— and tidier. It can make a bedroom appear very neat, even if nobody ever makes the bed.

Example of a Single-Bed Design
This design is by Van Staeyen Intérieur of Belgium, using a queen size bed, built-in shelves, and a cabinet.

Add a Disappearing Step
Build a step that pulls out of a drawer underneath the mattress. This provides easy access to the bed and disappears when not in use.

Designs by Johan van Staeyen. Photos by Luc Roymans.

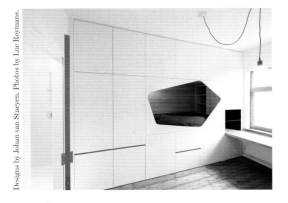

Inspired by Boat Designs

Make a Bed Cozy and Safe
A bed built into a wall creates an extracozy sleeping space to snuggle down and feel safe.

Design It as a Sitting Space
The bed may be only high enough to sit from the waist up, while your legs slide into an even lower space.

Make It Fun for the Kids
You can take an ordinary bedroom and convert it into a fun house for three adventurous children by carving out beds on three walls just like on a boat. The kids would have a great time crawling into their boat beds at night.

Example of a Triple-Bed Design
This design of three beds wedged into a very small space is by Jack Richens of thismovinghouse.com.

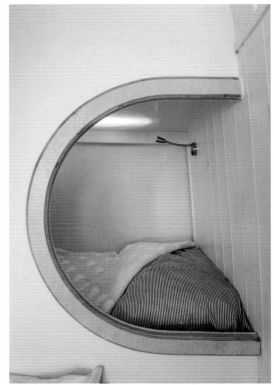

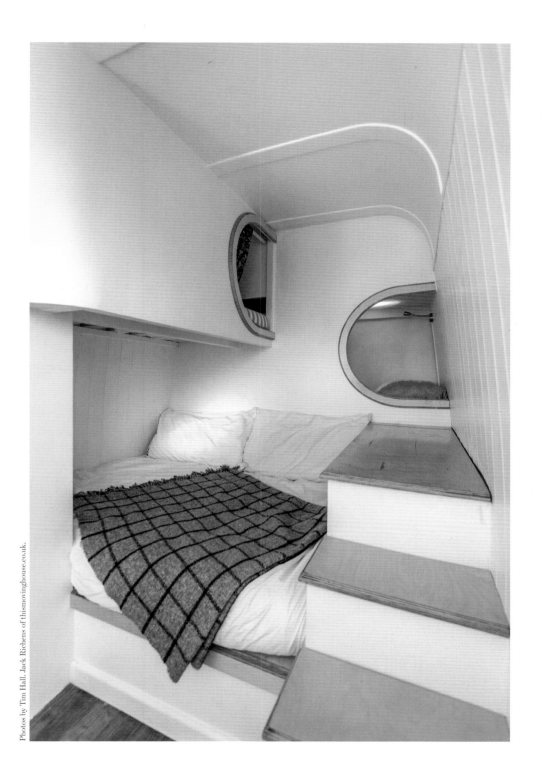

DRAWERS IN THE WALL

Borrow space from a closet.

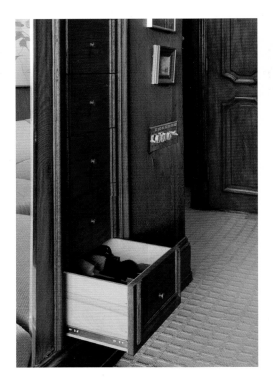

Look for "Dead" Corners

You may have a closet with a "dead" corner where two clothes rods cross, making it hard or even impossible to pull out a garment. This is a "dead" space.

Look outside the Closet

This "dead" corner isn't usually dead on the other side of the closet wall. Here the space may be fully accessible.

DIY Tips

First measure the inside of the closet to make sure you are using the entire corner space. Then carefully cut a hole through the wall to that exact measurement. (If you are using a ready-made drawer unit, you only have to cut the hole to fit the dimensions of the unit.)

Create a Design Feature

Wall drawers can be an attractive design feature, especially if the fronts match the surrounding molding, baseboard and cornice. If you use a molding around the drawer unit, you can get away with not having to re-finish the wall.

In my studio apartment, I have only two closets: one small and one large (at least for Manhattan): 4' x 5' (1.2m x 1.5m). The large one, however, was not very usable because it had hanging rods that crossed each other, with a dead space in between. So I hired a carpenter to build in seven drawers. It works perfectly. But to figure out what goes where in my seven drawers, I had to devise a system where I put my clothes away in the order of my putting them on: underwear on the bottom and headscarves on top. In between are my socks, tops, sweaters, and pants.

DRAWERS IN THE WALL

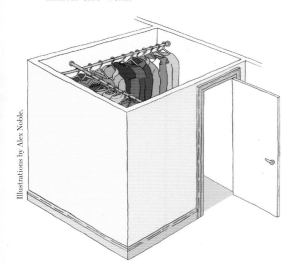

Illustrations by Alex Noble.

BEFORE

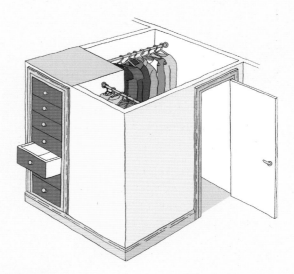

AFTER

7 FLOOR SPACES

A floor is more than a walkway.

Raise Floor Just a Few Inches

You don't need a high ceiling to create a raised floor platform. A change in floor level of just a few inches can provide storage, seating, and a separation of functions.

Gain Utility Space

Floor platforms are useful for air conditioning ducts, plumbing pipes, and electrical wiring.

Add Drama

Even a minor change in floor level gives an ordinary room a dramatic designer look.

PLATFORM AS SPACE DIVIDER

Define different functions.

Create a Division
A change in floor level is a subtle but effective way to separate spaces, such as dividing a sitting area from a dining area.

Build In Seating
Building in a sofa or settee at the side of a platform is a good way to close it up and divide the space.

Create Storage
Build storage in and around sofas and cabinets, with drawers on the sides and lids on the tops.

Roll Out a Bed
You can build in a bed where the legs fold inside the platform and drop down when the bed pulls out. You can provide storage for blankets and pillows alongside the bed.

Contrast the Floor Finishes
A change in floor finish can define different areas if you use soft surfaces like carpeting alongside hard surfaces like ceramic tiles.

illustration by Roberta Sandenbergh and Alex Noble.

@roberta.01

PLATFORM AS STORAGE

Hide beds, bicycles, and everything else.

DIY Tips

First you have to support the floor opening with short posts and beams. Then use plywood for the sides of the bin and the flap-top cover. Be sure to set your pull handles level with the floor, so you don't trip over them.

Order It Ready-made

Some suppliers such as Parador (see photo on opposite page) provide ready-made platforms with storage bins.

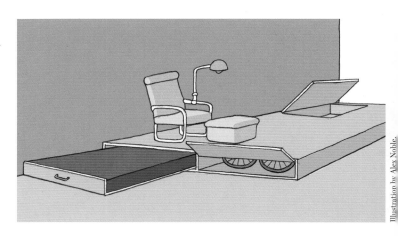

Illustration by Alex Noble.

MY STORY

I inherited a hollow floor platform when I bought my Manhattan studio apartment. It seemed a shame to waste so much potential storage space, so I hired a handyman to build a storage bin in the platform. The lift-up lid hides away old slides, CD's, photos, and notebooks. Covered with carpeting to match the rest of the apartment, the bin is concealed from view.

Photos by Adrian Wilson.

Design by Kathleen Kelly for Parador.

PLATFORM AS STORAGE

DRAWERS IN A PLATFORM

Combine drawer steps with seat.

Build Deep Drawers
Three steps up allows for plenty of drawer space.

Use Leftover Space as a Bench
The corner space can become a cozy seat.

Photos courtesy of Kasita.

MULTIPLATFORM STORAGE

Create drawers, bins, cabinets, and steps.

Put Shallow Drawers at the Bottom
This can be your first step—or, if it's too high, add a small step at midheight.

Add Flap-Up Bins to the Backs of the Drawers
The shallow drawers will leave room at the back for floor bins.

Finish Off with Door Swing Cabinets
Shelves behind swing doors at the back of the bins lead to the top.

Design by Studioata. Photo by Beppe Giardino.

BED IN A DRAWER

Make room for a play and work area.

Eliminate Cluttered Toy Depots

If you don't want your living room littered with toys, you get your kids to play in their bedrooms. But as the bedrooms get smaller and children get more toys, their rooms become cluttered toy depots, with little room to play or move around.

Create Magical Beds

Building a platform may seem like a lot of work for a toy-free living room. And, if you are renting, you may have to remove it when you move out. But for the decade or so while the kids are growing up, you will have provided your children with "magical beds" that disappear under the floor.

Adjust Mattress Size

Mattresses don't have to be a standard size. Have a piece of 4" (102mm)-foam cut out to suit your child's height.

Adjust Bed Size

When measuring for the bed drawer, leave enough height above the mattress for blankets and pillows to be strapped down.

Use Wheel Locks

Add wheel locks to the bed drawer, so the bed doesn't roll back while your child is still inside.

DIY

Make the platform frame from wood planks at least 12" (305mm) high with plywood or floorboards on top. Use as many floor supports as possible. Carpet the top and side of the platform.

Add Toy Bins

Use the space between the beds for lift-up storage bins—for toys, games, books, and school projects. Provide recessed metal pulls for the flap doors over the bins.

Closet-Desk Areas

For older kids, use the upper part of the platform as a closet-cum-desk area. Put a wood strip across the edge of the platform, so the chairs don't roll over the edge.

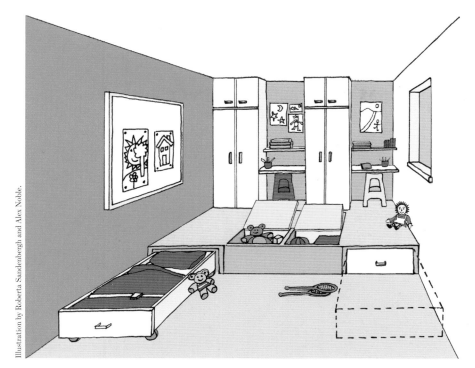

Illustration by Roberta Sandenbergh and Alex Noble.

Illustration by Hafiz Omer Shafiq.

BED IN A DRAWER

PLATFORM STEP BED

Add a cabinet to a bed space.

Gain a Space at the Side of the Bed
A bed on a raised platform not only gives you room for a full cabinet below, but also a large side space for books, magazines, and bedtime snacks.

DIY from Standard Units
This example is made from stock Ikea modules.

Photo Credit: Christopher Heider via HandyDadTV.

BEDSIDE PLATFORM DRAWER

Add storage for linen and blankets.

Use the Side of the Bed

Store your sheets, pillowcases, quilts, and blankets exactly where you need them.

Photo courtesy of Space Matters, Singapore.

8

WINDOW SPACES

A window is more than a lookout.

Windows are rarely center stage in a room, but they are still prime real estate. Don't overlook the opportunity to do more with these unique light-giving spaces:

Gain the Illusion of Extra Space

When you add a window to a room, the natural light and the glimpse of the outside world that comes through the glass make the room seem bigger.

Use the Window Frame Depth

The depth of a window frame—from the sill to the glass—easily accommodates a shelf or two. Many people use this to give their plants sunlight. But what about a dish rack, a drying rack, or a night table?

Extend the Window Inside

By jutting the window recess into a room—sometimes only a few extra inches—you can gain room for a bench, a desk, or even a dressing table.

Expand the Window Outside

By adding a bay window, you can add a settee, a table area, storage, or even a bathtub. With an outside railing, you can add a balcony.

DISH RACK IN A WINDOW

Let the sun dry your dishes.

Photo Credit: Passive Herb Watering, Bonnie Fortune, Brett Bloom, Copenhagen, 2011.

Fit a Plate Rack

This is for a window recess above a sink. Put the dishes in while they're wet and let them dry in the sunlight from the window. The rack will keep them from clicking and clacking against one another.

Use It Like a China Cabinet

Install several racks in the window frame, and you have a complete china cabinet, looking very decorative and leaving your wall cabinets free for other things.

Photo by D. Allen SA.

MY STORY

In my thatch cottage in South Africa, I installed a minikitchen in a corner of the living room. There wasn't room for a wall cabinet for dishes or even a shelf above the counter. But there was a small, narrow window above the sink. I bought a plastic plate rack and fit it right into the window recess. All my different-size plates fit into the rack, so it served as my one and only china cabinet. I let the dishes dry in the sunny window and took them out again only when I was ready to serve another meal.

DRYING RACK IN WINDOW

Use it as a blind when closed.

"Blindry"

This clever small space idea is by Kim Bobin and Ko Kyungeun, who called it the "Blindry." It won a 2011 Red Dot Design Award for its design concept.

Pulls Out from Window
The drying rack is installed in the window frame and pulls out as a drying rack when fully open.

Turns into Window Louvers
When closed, the unit serves as window louvers to keep out the sun.

Frees Up Storage Space
Because the unit remains in the window frame, it frees up the storage space normally reserved for the drying rack.

Acts as Legal Drying Area
This also keeps you out of trouble with local regulations against outdoor clotheslines, because all your clothes are inside, hanging from a window.

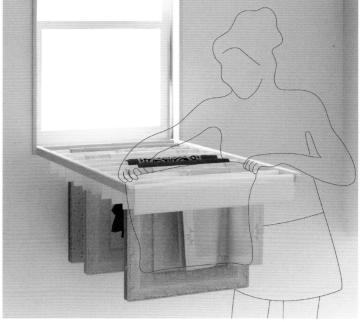

Product Photo courtesy Kim Bobin and Ko Kyungeun.

WINDOW IN A STORAGE BOX

Create storage all around a window.

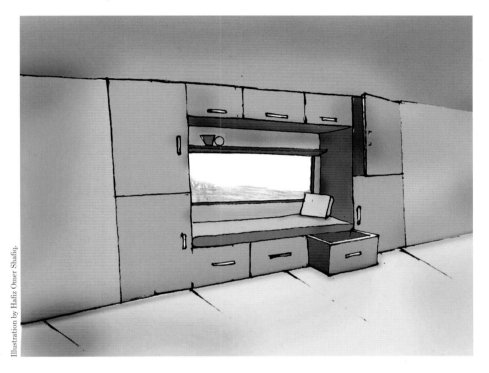

Illustration by Hafiz Omer Shafiq.

Wall with Closets and Window

This is for a room where your closets are placed on the same wall as a window.

Build a "Storage Box"

The idea is to build storage units and shelves above the window, drawers underneath it, and closets on the two sides.

Storage Forms a "Picture Frame"

The resulting 2' (610mm) deep "picture frame" around the window becomes an extension of the sill: a wall bench for sitting or lounging.

BALCONY IN A WINDOW

Your "lookout" becomes an outdoor space.

BALCONY IN A WINDOW

Photos courtesy of HofmanDujardin | Bloomframe®.

Apartment House Windows with "Bloomframe" Foldout Balconies

Apartments with Window/ Balconies

Some of the lucky occupants of this canal apartment house designed by architects HofmanDujardin in North Amsterdam have windows that fold out to become balconies.

When the weather is too cold to enjoy the outdoors, they keep the windows shut. When the warm weather arrives, they can crank them out for a place in the sun.

Install a Window Frame that Folds Out

The architects call their design *bloomframe*. It is a window frame that folds out to become a small outdoor space, strong enough for an adult to sit or stand.

Enjoy an Urban Dream

It is an urban dream to be able to open a window and, magically, have a balcony! Thanks to the Amsterdam architectural team Hofmandujardin, this is no longer just a dream.

This Could Be the Future of Cities

If local building departments in metropolitan areas begin to approve of this clever innovation, it could open up countless closed-in apartments all over the world, with a balcony to the outside world.

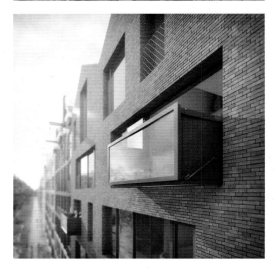

SETTEE IN A WINDOW

Add space and glamor to a small room.

This is one of the best ways to add space and light to a small room. It not only increases the size of a room, but also transforms it into a more elegant and inviting space.

Try to Get Permission

If you live in a multifamily dwelling, you will have to get permission from the owners of the building or the Board of Directors. Don't be put off by the application process. It takes time, but I eventually received permission to build four bay windows in my sectional title (condominium) apartment in Cape Town, South Africa.

If You Can't Get Permission

If you can't extend outward, you can still build a window seat toward the inside of your room to look like a bay window. Make the seat a maximum of 14" (356mm) deep, so it doesn't take up too much space.

Window Shades

Use the type of window shade that rolls upward from the sill. This way you can look out and avoid seeing your neighbor across the street.

Seat Corners

If your window seat extends beyond the walls, splay or round the corners of the seat to avoid bumping into them all the time.

Buy a Ready-made

Choose a ready-made bay window that more or less approximates the width of your existing window, so you don't have to break open more of the exterior wall. If it is smaller than the existing window, fill in the gap with concrete or cement and finish it with a color and material to match the existing walls.

Or Build One Yourself

You can have one custom-made or else make it a DIY project.

MY STORY

In my apartment in the South African city of Cape Town, I was able to fit three beds and two baths into 970 sq. ft. (90 sq. m.). The main bedroom was only 10' x 11' (3.048m x 3.353m) with a closet on one side of a queen-size bed, but no room for a chair or bench. Luckily, I was able to get permission from the Board of Directors to add a very shallow bay window to the outside of the building. This photo was the happy result.

Photo by Wieland Gleich.

Photos by Hamish Niven.

DRESSING TABLE IN A WINDOW

Do your makeup with natural light.

(a) Install a Deep Shelf at Table Height

This should jut out only slightly from the window recess. A mica finish is easy to clean.

(b) Install a Shelf Below

With a low window, this shelf can sit directly on the windowsill. This could also have a mica finish.

(c) Install Glass Shelves Above

These shelves are built right into the window frame above the dressing table and are much shallower than the table below.

(d) Use a Magnifying Mirror

Get one with a battery light so you don't need an electric plug.

(e) Add a Stool

Try to find a stool with a swivel base and an upholstered seat. Only when you're truly comfortable in your window niche are you ready to enjoy it.

(f) Keep your Makeup Neat

Nothing will be hidden. Your makeup sits permanently on the glass shelves in mugs and bowls, so try to be extra neat.

(g) Buy a Bottom-Up Window Shade

A window shade that stacks at the bottom and pulls upward will give you both privacy and the maximum amount of natural light. Ideally, you will be able to see the sky, not the building across the street.

MY STORY

Our Greenwich Village apartment was on the first floor of a beautiful old building on lower Fifth Avenue. It was small, only 800 square feet (74m²), cut down from a much larger apartment. But it had six large arched windows that came down almost to the floor. One window faced west toward Fifth Avenue, the other five faced south toward East 11th Street. One of these enormous windows was, a bit incongruously, in the bathroom. It was this window that became my dressing table, a lovely space that my indulgent husband built for me, carving it out from the deep recess. There was a partition covered with a bold flowered fabric to separate the dressing table from the rest of the bathroom. It was a beautiful light-filled space that became my private place to sit and dream.

Photo by John Sandenbergh.

DRESSING TABLE IN A WINDOW

NIGHT TABLE IN A WINDOW

Make room for a bed lamp.

Good for a Small Bedroom

This idea is for a bedroom so small that the bed is pushed up right against the window sill and there's no room for a side table.

Make It the Right Height

You have to be able to reach your book and turn off your reading lamp without getting out of bed, but the table can't be so low that it interferes with the blanket or duvet.

Make It the Right Length

Don't make it so long that you can't make up the bed from the window side.

DIY Tips

Cut a shelf the same width as the sill plus two extras to use as vertical supports. Glue the three shelves together and finish with stain and lacquer as desired. Screw one supporting shelf into the frame and the other into the sill with small steel angles.

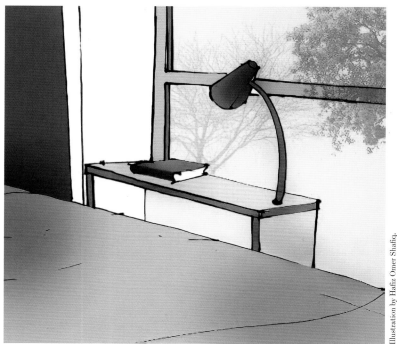

Illustration by Hafiz Omer Shafiq.

DESK IN A WINDOW

Push out the wall for a place to work.

Borrow Space from the Outside

When you need a big workspace and
have zero space inside, consider pushing
out the wall with a bay window to
borrow space from outside.

MY STORY

*The second bedroom in my new Cape Town apartment wasn't even
a bedroom. It was an extension of the living room, separated by shoji
screens* (see Chapter 3: Divided Spaces). *The space measured 9' x 10'*
(2.743m x 3.048m). *It had a queen-size bed, a closet, and room for
nothing else. When I finally got permission to push out the walls to install
bay windows in the apartment, I built a desk into this bonus space and
found a wonderful light-filled place to work right next to my bed.*

Photo by Hamish Niven.

BATHTUB IN A WINDOW

Enjoy a Jacuzzi in an extended space.

Use a Window that Folds Out

A window that extends out like the one below by Nana Wall Systems can open up your bath to an outside garden.

Or a Bay Window

In page 171's example, a side window reveals a view of the sea.

MY STORY

I pushed my luck with the Sectional Title Board in Cape Town and applied for permission to build a bay window in the bathroom. After three years, I was allowed only a very shallow extension, just enough to fit a bath into the window. I added a skylight, and, even with frosted glass for privacy, it was always full of light. A bonus was a view of the sea when I opened one of the side windows. This bathtub was on the opposite side of the world from my old Greenwich Village dressing table, but once again I found a place to dream inside a window frame.

Photo courtesy of Nana Wall Systems.

CEILING SPACES

A ceiling is more than an overhead.

Start Looking Up

Most of us never look up. Tilt your head back and see what's it like up there. Don't ignore the ceiling in your battle to expand your living space.

Use the Ceiling as a "Fifth Wall"

Think of the ceiling as a fifth wall, the last frontier in your battle to find more space. It's always available, but it's rarely used. You just have to change your mindset about using your ceilings.

Use It to Clear Your Floors

Ask yourself if some bulky item couldn't be supported from the ceiling or even hoisted up there. Your limited floor space has plenty of uses other than a lot of legs sticking out all over the place. And it's a lot easier to vacuum or sweep a floor without them.

Use It as a Theatrical Distraction

You can also think of your ceiling as a blank canvas to fill with theatrical effects like multiple levels, a painting, dramatic lighting, or a sculptural effect. Your visitors will be so charmed and distracted by what's up there, they won't even notice how small your apartment is.

BICYCLE ON THE CEILING
Hoist it up and pull it down.

Inexpensive and Available
With the growing popularity of bicycling comes the question of where to put your vehicle in a small apartment. The answer—at least for a bicycle that weighs less than 50 pounds—is a ceiling hoist. These are available from popular outlets like Amazon, Walmart, Home Depot, and others.

Install a Pulley inside an Apartment
You have to first find a supporting beam, which may mean opening up the ceiling and even reinforcing it.

Beware of Low Headroom
For a tall person, this may not be the best solution (see Chapter 6: Wall Spaces).

Photo courtesy of REI, Recreational Equipment Inc.

BABY FROM THE CEILING
Find space in a crowded apartment.

Use a Lightweight Bassinet

This may not be the first place you think of for your newborn baby, but if your floor is already crowded with cabinets and trunks and piles of baby clothes, the ceiling could be the perfect place to hang a lightweight bassinet.

DIY

Just rig up a hook and some rope and attach a fabric-lined basket or bassinet. A baby weighs so little you needn't worry about securing the bassinet to a structural beam.

Or Ready-made

Hussh-cradles offers attractive hanging bassinets for sale (one shown here).

Product Photo courtesy of Hussh-cradles.

BABY CARRIAGE ON THE CEILING

Clear the hallway.

Strollers can fold up and hang on a wall, but baby carriages are too bulky and remain a challenge for small spaces.

Find a Support
If you live in an apartment, get a handyman to find a structural beam in your ceiling to support a pulley or lift system.

Try a Bicycle Hoist
The pulley systems sold for bicycles will work for some carriages. You will need a lifting hook and a pulley block—plus the usual bolts, washers, and nuts.

Or a Platform Lift
For a hallway, a 3' x 3' (.9m x .9m) platform lift may work better than a bicycle hoist. You roll the carriage onto the platform, and then the whole thing can lift up to the ceiling in one go.

Check Your Headroom
If you are very tall or your ceiling is low, this is definitely not the solution for you.

Illustrations by hafiz Omer Shafiq.

TOYS ON THE CEILING

Keep kids' toys off the floor.

Use Baskets on Pulleys
For this clever small-space idea, use a hoist to pull toys up to the ceiling and down again.

DIY
All you need are a few baskets (or pails), some light pulleys, and handles on the wall.

Fun for Kids
The kids will love pulling the baskets up and down and can make tidying up their toys a fun exercise.

TABLE ON THE CEILING

Clear the decks and have a party.

For a Party, Meeting, or Classroom

There comes a time when we all wish we had a spare room with a clear floor area. This might be for a party, a club meeting, children's games, or even a yoga class.

Hoist a Table and Hang Up the Chairs

Try hoisting your dining table up to the ceiling and hanging your chairs on the wall. (See Chapter 6: Wall Spaces.) Then turn on the music and dance!

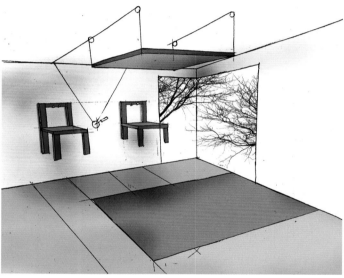

Illustrations by Hafiz Omer Shafiq.

DESK ON THE CEILING

Hoist it away after working hours.

Office Desks Automatically Lift at 6 p.m.

An Amsterdam architectural office (ZECC Architects) figured out how to get their employees to stop working after hours. All the desks are connected to a pulley system on a timer. At 6 p.m., they are automatically lifted up to the ceiling. In the morning, they come down again.

Or Lift Your Laptop from Your Bed

Many people like to work on their laptops in bed. One man rigged a pulley to lift his desk up and down from his bed. When finished with working, he just closes his laptop and hoists up the desk. (See photo bottom right.)

Design by ZECC Architects. Photography by JRimageworks.

Photo courtesy of Matt Silver.

BED ON THE CEILING

Free up at least 30 square feet.

Get Rid of Your Bed
Your limited floor space has plenty of other uses.

DIY
This could be a project for a handy person using eyehooks, lag screws, pulleys, ropes, or fabric tapes to hoist up your bed when it's not in use.

Ready-made
There are many manufactured ceiling hoist beds on the market. The one shown here is a sliding system by Espace Loggia:

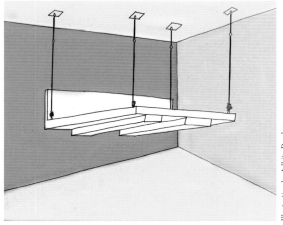

Illustration by Adhita Razdan.

Photo courtesy of Espace Loggia.

SOFA ON THE CEILING

Keep the floor dust-free.

For Cleanliness

All sofas collect masses of dust underneath. So you may prefer to have a clear floor under the sofa. It could swing like a porch divan or stay perfectly still—your choice.

For Special Occasions

There are occasions like home weddings or bar mitzvahs when you want your furniture out of the way. Instead of calling in a moving van, you could hoist them up to the ceiling.

Photo courtesy of Paola Lenti.

SOFA ON THE CEILING

CHAIR ON THE CEILING

Swing and twirl around.

Basket Chairs

There are many styles of hanging basket chairs on the market like this one by Sestini & Corti. Besides leaving the floor clear, they also impart a casual air to a room, and you can even twirl around.

Design by Sestini & Corti

SCULPTURE ON THE CEILING

Glamorize your space.

Add Drama

If you want to use your "fifth wall"—the ceiling—to the absolute max, think of creating a large sculptural effect. It can add theater and have such a dramatic impact that nobody will notice how small your apartment really is.

DIY Tips

Start with installing a ceiling light fixture. Add wallpaper with a dark design all around the light. Then draw an abstract design on gypsum board and cut it out. Hold up your design to the ceiling and move it around until it looks right and, finally, nail, glue, or staple it to the ceiling on top of the wallpaper. Then paint. Even if it isn't perfect, it will still look dramatic and should elicit a chorus of "Wow"s from your guests.

Photo courtesy of Zaha Hadid Architects and ZM-PR.

POSTERS ON THE CEILING

Think of the Sistine Chapel.

Transform a Room

A blown-up photo or print can transform an ordinary room into a dramatic world of fantasy and imagination.

DIY for Decals

Large decals do not need glue, paste, or any special chemicals: they come with a self-adhesive backing. You simply peel off and apply. The decals can be applied to all smooth surfaces with a plastic squeegee.

DIY for Artwork

If your artwork is heavy (as opposed to paper-thin), try to attach it directly to a ceiling support or rafter. Avoid heating ducts or wires.

Show Off a Collection

Put up your collection of playbills, prints, or posters. The ceiling may be the only place in your home big enough to hold them all. Colorful posters on the ceiling will add theatrical drama to what was originally an ordinary space.

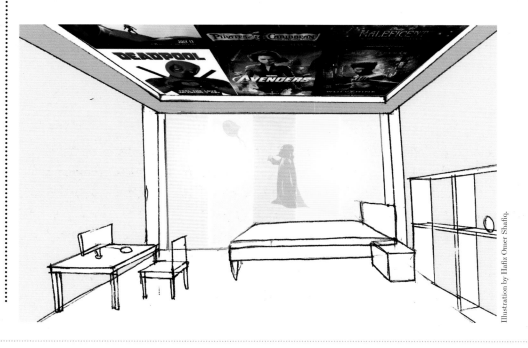

Illustration by Hafiz Omer Shafiq.

MY STORY

I once held a Cousins Party where fifty-two of my cousins came to New York, some from as far away as California. When they arrived, they found themselves surrounded by life-size blowups of old black-and-white photos of the family. I also mounted an enormous family tree diagram on a poster board. It was a very dramatic effect and a wonderful party. Afterward, I didn't have enough wall space for the poster boards in my small apartment, so I put them up on the ceilings of my closets. Now, every time I open my closet doors, I get a chance to visit with my family!

LIGHTING ON THE CEILING
Make it look theatrical.

Start with Recessed Lights
A strong ceiling design using recessed lights will have a good overall impact.

Add Sculptural Effect
Varying the heights of a gypsum board ceiling will emphasize your lighting design.

Add Hidden Fluorescent Lights
The glow of light above a dropped ceiling will be a dramatic addition.

Interiors by Sager & Associates. Photography by Wieland Gleich.

SPLIT-LEVEL CEILING

Gain illusion of height.

Lower Part of the Ceiling
This will create a cozy effect above a space without a window, especially with fluorescent lights installed above it.

Raise Another Part of the Ceiling
This will create a dramatic feeling of height, especially next to a window.

MY STORY

The living room of my renovated apartment in Cape Town was designed with two different ceiling heights: a low section with recessed fluorescent lights in the middle of the room, a high section near the window. This simple technique adds enormously to the drama of the room.

Interiors by Sager & Associates. Photography by Wieland Gleich.

EMPTY SPACES

Waiting for you to find them.

Untapped Resources

You probably have no idea how many untapped spaces you have in your home. Think about those empty corners, the space above your stove or toilet, even the half-inch behind some furniture—all that space can be used to add more storage and functionality. It's time to look at your home with fresh eyes to discover unused or underutilized spaces.

Look for Leftover Spaces:
- Above a desk.
- Above a hallway.
- Above a door.
- Above a window.
- Under a staircase.
- Under a bed.
- Under a table.
- Under an overhang.
- Behind a desk.
- Behind a door.

Look for Underutilized Spaces:
- The side of a cabinet.
- The inside of a cabinet door.

Make Spaces Work Harder

Remember that space is money. Stretch those dollars by making your spaces work as hard as possible for you.

Make Successful Marriages

Team up unused or underutilized spaces with things that you need: a bookcase, a bed, a chest of drawers, or even a bathroom.

BED OVER HALLWAY

Use a space nobody notices.

Hidden in Plain Sight

This is probably the least noticeable space in your house or apartment. People walk through a front door and are past the entry area before they even know where they are. Nobody looks up. That's what makes this a great place for a bed. It's hidden away.

You May Need to Increase the Headroom

You need at least 4' (1219mm) to sit up in bed, and you may not have even that much height. But hey, it's just a place to sleep—especially if you're young and athletic and thrilled to be living on your own.

(a) Lower the Hallway Ceiling

Hallways are not considered a living space under most building codes, so you can lower a hallway ceiling to a 6'–8" (2m) door height.

(b) Use Closets Underneath

If you want your sleeping area lower to the floor, put the bed over 5' (1.5m)- or 6' (1.8m)-tall closets.

Easy to Build DIY

Entry halls are not very wide, so you don't require a complicated structure. A handyman with average skills can put up posts and beams on the walls, deck braces and floor joists, plus a plywood floor and an easy-climb ladder.

Don't Forget a Railing

Even if you are planning to sleep there by yourself, be safe. You could easily roll out of bed or wake up out of a dream and forget where you are.

BED OVER HALLWAY

Illustrations by Hafiz Omer Shafiq.

MY STORY

When I was living on 11 acres of countryside between Pretoria and Johannesburg, I converted old store rooms, garages, stables, and servants' quarters into rental cottages. I replaced the corrugated metal roofs with high-pitched thatch roofs, allowing me to design sleeping lofts over the bathrooms, minikitchens, and bedrooms. I always thought of my little cottages as "Soho Lofts under Thatch." When I started a computer design business in Johannesburg, I offered free training for dealers on the weekends. The classes were held at my property out in the country. As an extra perk, I allowed out-of-town dealers to sleep over in the cottages, which had sleeping lofts. I had a dealer from Windhoek, Namibia, who slept in a loft that didn't have a railing. He got up suddenly in the middle of the night, didn't know where he was, and fell off the balcony. We were lucky that he didn't break his neck, sue me, or both!

NEXT TO THE TOILET

Grab a few inches next to the toilet.

Stop Leaning over the Sink

A toilet seat already gives you a place to sit down, so you don't have to stand and lean over the sink to use the mirror on the medicine cabinet.

Stop Putting Things Away

Keep your stuff permanently on the shelves, including the creams that you normally keep in the medicine cabinet. This way, you won't have to empty your makeup bag (or shaving kit) onto the countertop every day.

Make Your Routine a Pleasure

This is not just about finding a place to put on makeup. It is about making your daily routine a pleasure, with everything in place and organized exactly as you like it.

Look For an Overhang

Sink countertops sometimes have a small overhang. Fit a narrow shelf unit underneath to grab a few extra inches. The one shown here, next to a toilet seat, became my dressing table.

Buy a Ready-made

Look for a ready-made metal shelf unit (usually about 30" or 762mm high) that will fit nicely underneath the sink top.

Photo by Adrian Wilson.

MY STORY

This dressing table-cum-vanity sink is from my Manhattan studio apartment. I got tired of leaning over the sink to do my makeup in the medicine cabinet mirror. I saw an opportunity in the overhang next to the toilet and looked for a shelf unit that would fit underneath. The rest is history. Now, every time I use this previously empty space—which is just about every day—I have a great big smile on my face.

Magnifying Mirror

(a)

You will find a magnifying mirror with a battery-operated built-in light indispensible. Also, see Chapter 8: Window Spaces.

Sit Sideways

(b)

Sit sideways on the toilet seat with the lid down. Get a thick toilet seat cover.

Illustration by Roberta Sandenbergh and Alex Noble.

STORAGE IN A BATHTUB

In between tub and the surround.

A Lot of Wasted Space

This empty space could hold all your shampoos, conditioners, loofas, bath brushes, bath salts, bath gels, bubble bath, body creams, razors, and even some candles. If you have the room, you could probably store your bathroom cleaning materials in there, as well.

Waiting For a Manufacturer

All you need is someone to build it for you—while you wait for a clever bath fixture company to start selling it as an optional extra.

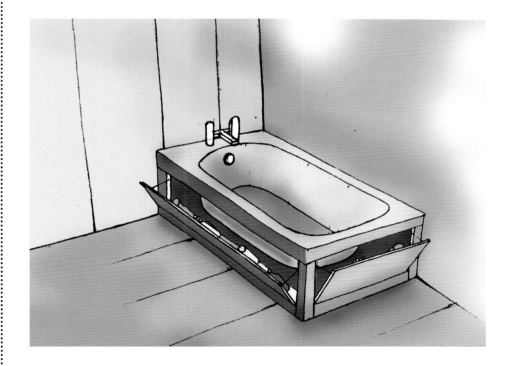

TOILET UNDER A STAIRWAY

Unearth a hidden room.

Ultrapractical Use of an Empty Space

You can easily fit a small wall-mounted basin and a toilet.

Check Out Municipal Requirements

You must provide an air vent and enough slope for the toilet to drain. For this, you may have to provide a step at the door. (For more useful hints, refer to Chapter 1: Bathroom in a Closet.)

Illustrations by Hafiz Omer Shafiq.

IDEA 93.

STUDY UNDER A STAIRWAY

Create a cozy hideaway.

All the Desk Space You Need
Just move your desk under a stairway to find a cozy place to work.

Hide Yourself Away
You can really get things done here, especially if nobody knows where you are hiding.

Add Light and Shelves
Perhaps an L-shaped work area, a desk lamp, and some shelves over the desk.

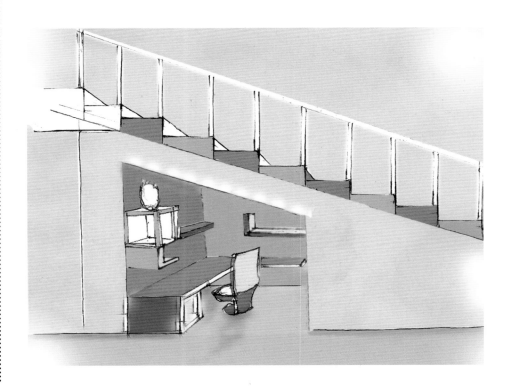

WALK-IN CLOSET UNDER STAIRWAY

Get rid of your "catch-all."

Rip out That Single Door

A single door closet under a stairway often becomes a "catch-all" for broken furniture and old sports equipment. "Out of sight" often evolves into "out of mind" and it can become a hard-to-get-at disorganized mess.

Install Fold-Out Doors

With custom-built doors that fold away, this can become the closet of your dreams—everything visible, everything organized, and everything easy-to get-at.

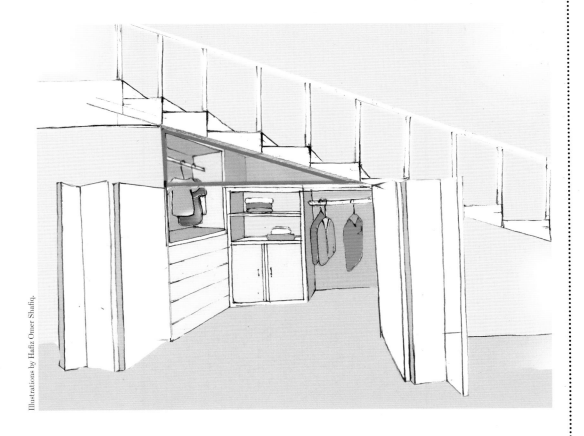

Illustrations by Hafiz Omer Shafiq.

BINS UNDER STAIRWAY

Measure them to fit perfectly.

Measure and Make

Try to use every inch of these awkward spaces with containers that open up or pull out. You will probably have to enlist a carpenter or handyman to get your bins to fit your space exactly.

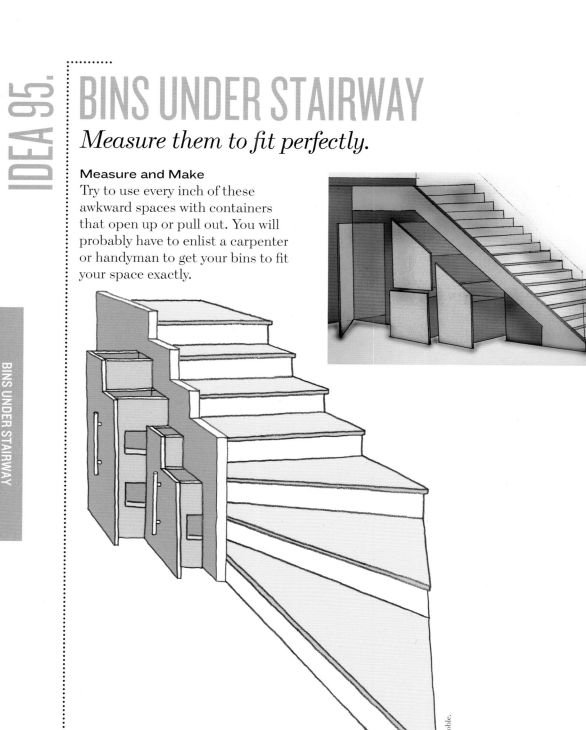

Illustration by Hafiz Omer Shafiq.

Illustration by Alex Noble.

DRAWERS IN STEPS

Gain an extra chest of drawers.

Using steps as a chest of drawers is one of those small-space ideas so simple and obvious that when you first see it, you'll say to yourself, "Why didn't I think of this before?"

If you are building or renovating
Include this detail in the specifications for the stairs. It will be a lot cheaper than changing them later on.

If you have an existing stairway
Convert one step at a time when you need the storage and have some extra cash. A clever handyman could easily do the conversion.

Illustration by Hafiz Omer Shafiq.

DRAWERS UNDER CABINETS

Make use of "dust catchers."

Good for cabinets with space at the bottom

Buy a drawer slide and get hold of your handyman to install it for you at the bottom of a cabinet. You may have to be use epoxy to hold it in place. Then get him to make a drawer to fit.

Good for your "flat" kitchen items

Trays, cutting boards, and cookie sheets will find a good home under a cabinet.

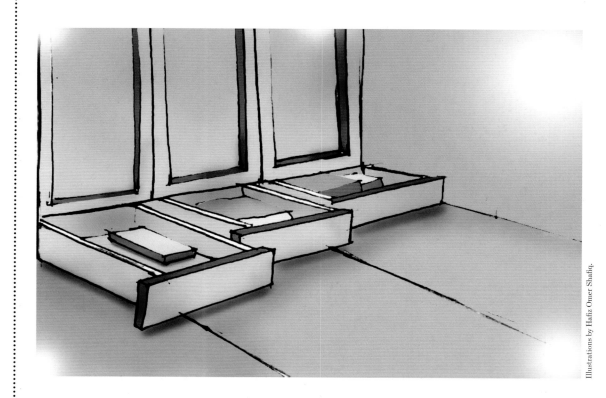

Illustrations by Hafiz Omer Shafiq.

STORAGE UNDER BED
There's lots of space down there.

Answer to a Cluttered Room

Drawers under a bed are especially useful as toy bins in a kid's room. You can paint them yourself and teach your child about colors and letters while keeping his or her room tidy.

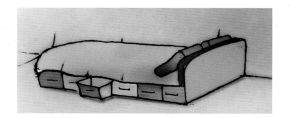

Courtesy of Baxton Studio.

Like a Horizontal Closet

Think of the space under a bed as a full-sized closet—only it's horizontal. The amount of space is enormous, and it's a crime to waste any of it. A tilt-up bed will give you the maximum amount of storage.

MY STORY

When my husband and I decided to travel through Europe in a camper van with our 4-year-old daughter, we used deep cardboard file drawers (see Chapter 1: Closet Spaces) to fit under the van's slide-out bed that we designed ourselves. The drawers held a wealth of stuff—shoes, underwear, jeans, shirts, pajamas, towels—in fact, everything we took with us on the trip. Every once in a while, we found a laundromat or a laverie automatique, *and we emptied out the drawers (plus the curtains, sheets, and blankets) into a row of washing machines and waited in our shorts while everything got clean. Then we put it all back again. We traveled for almost two years, until our daughter was ready to start school. It felt wonderful to have so few possessions to worry about. We felt we had stumbled upon a surprisingly simple, inexpensive, and utterly happy way of life!*

MIRRORED SPACES

Make use of a small home's best friend.

Change Your "Mirror Mindset"

People often avoid using mirrors to make their small houses look bigger because they think mirrored walls are tacky and old-fashioned. Wrong. Yes, mirrors on bedroom ceilings are tacky. Yes, gold leaf-framed mirrors are old-fashioned. But nothing will expand your space faster than a mirrored wall.

Make a Room Look Larger

A large mirror in a small room will double, triple, or quadruple the size of the room.

Change How a Space Feels

You transform a room and make it more interesting by adding the reflection of another space.

Light Up a Room

Whenever mirrors reflect a window or light fixture, they make a room seem lighter and brighter.

Fool the Eye

Who is to say what is real and what is not? You often cannot tell the difference. In fact, it may be hard not to believe what your eyes are telling you.

MIRROR A SIDEWALL

See everything double.

Mirror the Wall against a Sofa
This is a great trick to increase your space:

(a) The sofa looks twice as long.

(b) One lamp becomes two lamps.

(c) One painting becomes two paintings.

MIRROR A WINDOW

Extend your view outward and upward.

Enlarge the Room
Mirrors at the sides of the window—or window wall—will make the room look wider.

Increase the Light
With mirrors at the sides of a window, the light from the outside will come into your room.

Reflect the Scene
When you mirror a ceiling panel directly above a window, it will not only make the room look higher, but it will also reflect the scene outside.

Photos by Adrian Wilson.

MIRROR A VIEW
See outside from inside.

Nothing Is What It Seems
You may have to touch the walls to know what you are looking at in the photo below. It's only a blank wall reflecting a view of a balcony and another wall reflecting a fireplace on the other side of a table.

(a) Balcony Illusion
What you are looking at is a blank wall reflecting a view seen only from the perspective of the photographer.

(b) Fireplace Illusion
What you are looking at is a blank wall at the side of the dining table. There is only one table and one fireplace.

(c) Bed Illusion
Mirrored panels form the bed partition, so you see the view from both sides of the bed!

Photos by Adrian Wilson.

MY STORY

My Manhattan studio is only 500 sq. ft (46 sq. m.), but it faces an 843-acre garden called Central Park. I was determined to see the park from everywhere in the apartment. I mirrored the ceiling and sidewalls near the window to extend the view upward and outward. I mirrored the opposite wall so I could see the view's reflection. I mirrored the backs of panels—including the inside of a Murphy bed partition—so that when they open, they reflect the reflection. It was a lot of work and a lot of mirrors, but I am now able to see the view just about everywhere I look.

MIRROR A BATHTUB

Create a luxurious spa.

Make Your Bathroom Extraordinary
The smallest, most ordinary bathroom will suddenly seem superluxurious when you install a floor-to-ceiling mirror.

Multiply Small Details
An unusual bath fitting, a recessed shelf, a planter—they will all be more noticeable by being shown twice.

Designed by Sofia Joelsson Design Studio.

MIRROR A CEILING

Transform a room.

Gain Higher Ceiling Height
With a mirrored ceiling in your living room, your guests will swear you have at least a 20-foot ceiling.

Add an Illusion
People will not comprehend exactly what they are looking at overhead.

Receive a Chorus of "Wow"s
You will deserve this reaction to the sheer drama of your overhead reflection. This is especially true when you add a floor-to-ceiling mirrored wall as in the photo below.

Photo courtesy of the Mandarin Oriental Hotel Barcelona.

12

MULTIPURPOSE FURNITURE

Buy two for the space of one.

Enjoy the Space
With a "2-for-1" piece of furniture, you can enjoy a 100 percent increase in your living space.

Enjoy the Choice
With today's shrinking living spaces, there's a big demand—and many more choices—for furniture that serves more than one purpose.

Enjoy the Discovery
Share my buzz of pure joy whenever I discover a clever new space-saving idea.

Keep Up-To-Date
When you are about to buy a new piece of furniture, find out which multipurpose versions of the same function are currently on the market.

Know That Models Change
You may find that some models shown here are no longer available.

SOFA INTO BUNK BEDS

Pop up two bunk beds.

A very clever sofa from **resourcefurniture.com** pulls up and out to become two bunk beds, complete with a built-in ladder.

Terrific for Kids—But Not Too Shabby for Adults

The two "bunks" are really full-sized beds, so adults could use them as well. Just think of Cary Grant and Eva Marie Saint on the train in Alfred Hitchcock's *North by Northwest*!

MY STORY

When my daughter, Margot, and her new husband, Martin, moved into a Manhattan studio apartment, they had to accommodate his two daughters who visited from France. Margot rushed to Resource Furniture on Third Avenue to order this clever sofa. But there wasn't enough time to ship a new unit from Italy, so she bought the showroom model. Since then, the disappearing bunk beds have made for many happy memories of the girls' visits to New York.

Photos by Adrian Wilson.

SOFA INTO TABLE AND SEATS

Pop up a table for six.

Who would suspect that a modest sofa could pull out to become a table for six?

Here's how it works:

1. Push down the back of the sofa.
2. Pull out the six cushions.
3. Pull down the fold-up legs.
4. Fold out the table.

This design, one of the cleverest space-savers ever, is by Konenkoid, a Ukranian-Polish studio.

Photos by Julia Kononenko, Studio "Kononenko ID."

CABINET INTO TABLE

Pull out when guests arrive.

Ready for Guests

You can quickly pull out this table from Stakmore with no need to store the leaves in a closet.

Use for Storage

When not being used as a table, the cabinet has room for trays, cutlery, and place mats.

Photos courtesy of of Stakmore Company.

CABINET INTO BED

Pull out a low "Murphy" bed.

No High Wall for a Murphy Bed
Some clever manufacturers such as Arason Enterprises have figured out how to stuff a Murphy bed into a well-designed low cabinet (shown here).

No Furniture in Front of Cabinet
There's less stuff to move out of the way when you pull out a bed from a cabinet, than with a sofa bed or a wall bed. This is because you don't usually keep a piece of furniture in front of a cabinet.

Match the Style of Your Furniture
You can blend the style of the cabinet to match the decor of your room.

Photos courtesy of Arason Enterprises.

DESK INTO BED

Roll down a place to sleep.

A clever design from *resourcefurniture.com* allows you to push a bed up, while a desk adjusts to its normal height. When you pull the bed down, the desk tucks away under the bed.

Use It for a Tiny Bedroom
Having just one piece of furniture as both your bed and your desk will make your small room look larger and more inviting.

Use It for a Roommate
I can see this idea working if you are sharing an apartment, especially if you have only part of a room (or an alcove) to yourself.

Use It for a Minimal Lifestyle
This is a good way to have both your day and night activities fit into a very small space with just a single piece of furniture. There's no need to pack up your desk even when you want to take a nap!

Courtesy of Clei/Resource Furniture.

CUPBOARD INTO TABLE

Pull out for a banquet.

Ready for a Feast

You can have a sit-down dinner for your whole family at Thanksgiving with this clever design by Nobuhiro Teshima: it folds out from a cabinet on wheels that can roll out to wherever you want it.

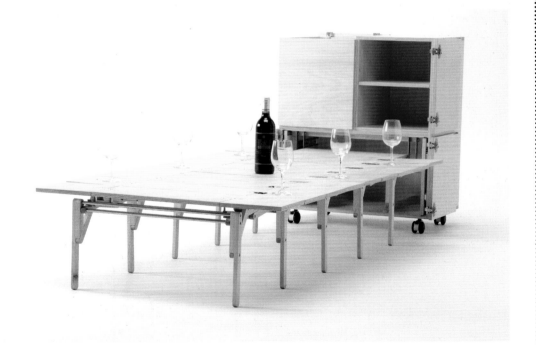

Photos courtesy of Nobuhiro Teshima.

COFFEE TABLE INTO DINING

Pop up a table.

In a small apartment, you used to have to choose between a dining table and a coffee table. No longer. With this clever design by *resourcefurniture. com*, you can pull a table up for dining and push it down again for coffee.

Use It to Eat Alone
You're all set for dinner on a coffee table.

Use It for Company
Add some chairs and pull up the same table for dining.

Product photos courtesy of resourcefurniture.com.

COFFEE TABLE INTO DESK

Pull up a place to work.

Ideal for an Urban Single Lifestyle:

- Order takeout.
- Sit on the sofa and eat on the coffee table.
- Clear the table and pull up the desk.
- Get out your laptop.
- Work until you fall asleep on the sofa.

Photo courtesy of Hayneedle Inc.

COFFEE TABLE INTO SEATS

Pull out a place to sit down.

Use It for Snacks or Drinks
Whether it's "tea for two" or
"four rosés for four," this is an
excellent way to entertain guests
in a small space.

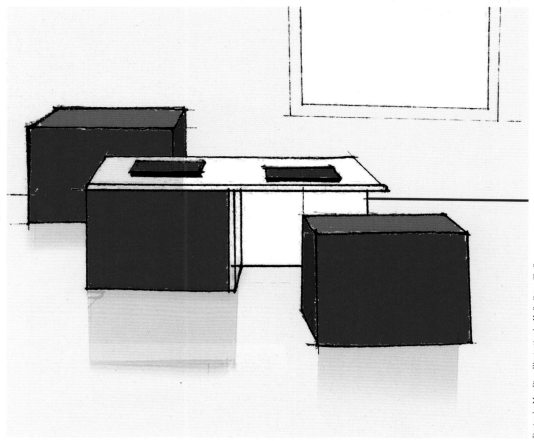

Design by Max Piva. Illustration by Hafiz Omer Shafiq.

BOOK INTO SEATS

Store extra seats on a shelf.

Called **bookniture**, this clever idea found in a **MOMA** catalog consists of cardboard stools that fold up into a book.

Ideal for Extra Guests
Having to seat extra people in a small apartment? Just take a few books down from the shelf and your problem is solved!

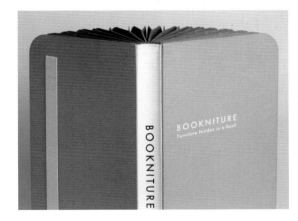

Photos courtesy of Bookniture

BIKE RACK INTO DESK

Park and work in the saddle.

A bicycle takes up a lot of space in a small apartment, so my usual advice is to hang it on a wall, hoist it to the ceiling, or push it under a floor platform. But what if it can double as a desk?

Use It to Study
You may get your best ideas while your body is in motion!

Use It to Exercise
This gives you a chance to exercise at home while doing some of your deskwork.

Buy It Ready-made
This clever design called a "pit in table" is available from Store Muu.

Photos courtesy of Store Muu.

INSTANT EAT-IN KITCHEN

Pull out a table and stools.

Apartments with "eat-in kitchens" are fast vanishing from urban real estate. A typical apartment kitchen nowadays has just a counter or two without space for a table. This clever design by BOX15 (UK) provides a solution.

Single-Counter Kitchen
The idea is best suited for this situation. You just pull out the table and stools and sit down.

Double-Counter Kitchen
Here it may be a bit tricky. The pull out table would always be useful as extra counter space, but the stools may be in the way for a "sit-down."

Pass-Through Kitchen
Here the "pull outs" go on the other side of the kitchen wall. The table and stools pull out from the kitchen cabinet through the wall. A bit tricky but more comfortable than perching on bar stools and eating at a counter!

Photos courtesy of BOX15UK. Product: T-ABLE & T-BENCH.

By the time you have reached this last page, dear readers, you may be overwhelmed by the many choices and opportunities I have given you to increase the space in your homes. I do hope you will make use of at least some of them.

But, most of all, you mustn't lose sight of the reason you are doing all of this: to have a home you truly want to live in. By all means, consolidate and compact and make your homes as cozy and efficient as possible. But please remember to leave some open spaces to move around in or just to look at. Too lean a space may cramp your spirit.

In a boat, everything fits very tight, and there is absolutely no space to spare. But the boat occupants can go up on deck and see the vast sky and open sea all around them. Make sure you have left some room in your homes to sit and stare—and even dance around!

If you have questions about your living spaces, you can go to the Q&A section on my website: www. smallspacearchitect.com. It may take a while to receive an answer, but I will do my best to get back to everyone who goes there and fills out a form.

Roberta Sandenbergh,
the small-space architect.

ACKNOWLEDGMENTS

To my late architect-husband, John, who gave me my first lesson in small-space living when we renovated our little 800-square-foot (74-square-meter) apartment in Greenwich Village so it could accommodate an architectural studio in the kitchen and a baby in a closet. I continued to learn from him when we built Daisy Belle together: a bright-orange VW camper van with a kitchen that folded out in back and a seat that slid out to become a double bed. I only wish he could have lived long enough to share my other small-space adventures.

To my brilliant daughter, Margot, without whom there would be no book. I would still be filling notebooks with my small-space ideas and occasionally writing a column about them. She not only encouraged me to produce this book, but also acted as my editor, agent, and general life adviser.

ABOUT THE AUTHOR

Roberta Sandenbergh is a Brooklyn-born architect who wound up living in South Africa with her 6-year-old daughter after her South African-born husband died on his way back to his native country.

In South Africa, Roberta used her New York smarts in designing small spaces to carve out a career for herself in small-scale residential design. One of her projects, a retirement community, won the annual Johannesburg Civic Design Award; two of her houses were featured in *Garden & Home* and *Habitat*.

Her love for condensing space led to a passion for computer-aided design. Roberta became the sub-Saharan representative for AutoCAD, a U.S.-based software product. She travelled all over Africa, spreading the word about this new technology, appointing resellers, and setting up training centers.

The author has written many illustrated columns on space-saving ideas. They have appeared in the *SA City Life* and *Home Handyman* magazines, as well as the *Johannesburg Star*, the *Washington Post* (Design Notebook series), and the *San Francisco Chronicle*. She has also written a book about what it was like to be an American living under apartheid.

She studied at Vassar College and received a B.Arch. from Pratt Institute. She also studied for a Masters in Urban Design at Witwatersrand University in Johannesburg.

Roberta says of herself: "I often waste time, and I sometimes waste money. But I absolutely hate to waste space."

INDEX